INDIVIDUALIZED SCIENCE INSTRUCTIONAL SYSTEM

PLANTS INDOORS

ANNOTATED TEACHER'S EDITION

Ginn and Company

A XEROX EDUCATION COMPANY

The work presented or reported herein was supported by a grant from the National Science Foundation. However, the opinions expressed herein do not necessarily reflect the position or policy of the National Science Foundation, and no official endorsement by that agency should be inferred.

Ginn and Company
A Xerox Education Company
Home Office: Lexington, Massachusetts 02173
0—663-33626—0

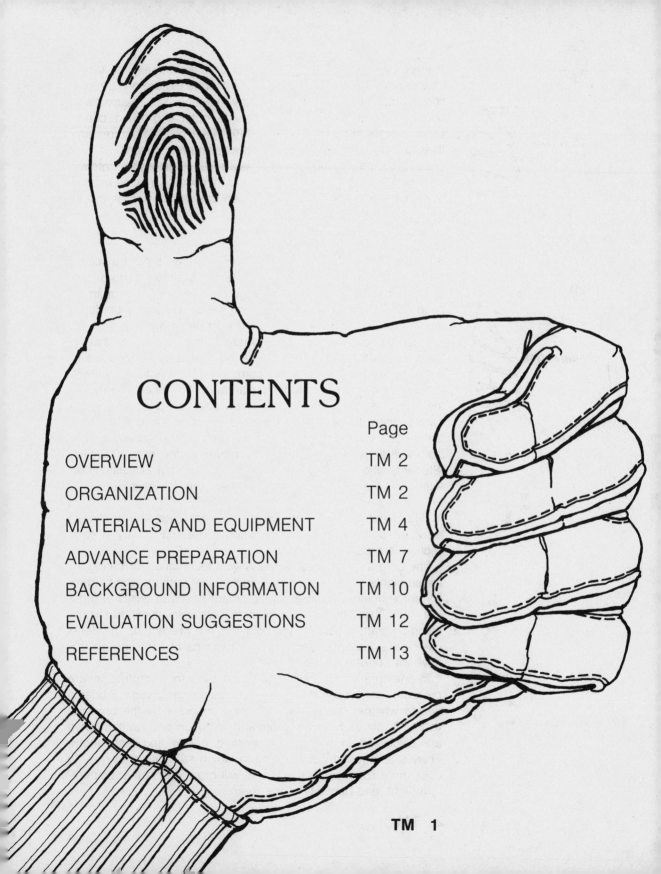

CONTENTS

	Page
OVERVIEW	TM 2
ORGANIZATION	TM 2
MATERIALS AND EQUIPMENT	TM 4
ADVANCE PREPARATION	TM 7
BACKGROUND INFORMATION	TM 10
EVALUATION SUGGESTIONS	TM 12
REFERENCES	TM 13

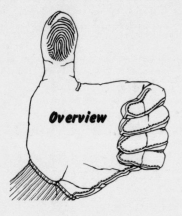

Overview

Plants Indoors presents information and techniques for taking care of house plants: getting new plants from mature ones, repotting plants, keeping plants healthy, treating sick plants, and choosing plant locations that provide optimal growing conditions. *Plants Indoors* also deals with major plant structures and their functions and with photosynthesis and respiration.

Since the care of house plants is a timely topic and of interest to many people, some activities in this minicourse may be used in home economics and adult education classes as well as in science classes.

Organization

Because of the special nature of this minicourse, it may be necessary for students to do some activities out of order: to do an excursion or advanced activity before a core activity. The chart on page TM 3 shows the order in which the activities may be done. Refer to the chart while reading the next paragraph.

If potting soil is not available, students may make their own in Excursion Activity 17. Thus, it may be necessary for students to do Excursion Activity 17 before completing Core Activity 2 (where potting soil is used). If students plan to do Advanced Activity 14, they are directed to begin immediately after completing Core Activity 2; then they return to the core activities. And if students plan to do Excursion Activity 19, they are directed to begin immediately after Activity 2; then they return to the core activities. (Students who don't do Activity 2 should also make decisions on Activities 14 and 19 before doing other core activities.)

In this minicourse there are eleven core activities, four advanced activities, and five excursion activities. The first activity in each section is a planning activity.

The core activities deal primarily with techniques for caring for house plants. Students learn to make stem cuttings and to identify some common house plants. Plant needs in terms of fertilizer, light, heat, water, and humidity are discussed, and some common plant problems and solutions are presented. Students use coleus plants to study the relationships of light and chlorophyll with photosynthesis.

In one core activity, historical experiments for phototropism are presented and observations and conclusions are given. Students decide whether the conclusions are supported by the observations. In another activity, normal distribution and normal curve are discussed in relation to seedling height and leaf length. There's a required core activity in which students plan how to decorate a room using plants that will grow well in the temperature, light, and humidity of the room.

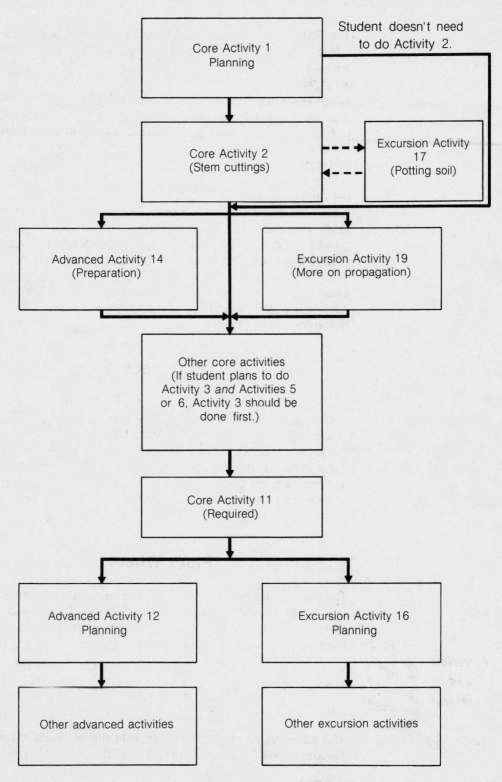

The *Plant Directory*, supplied separately, is used with Core Activities 2, 3, 5, 6, and 7. The directory presents some common house plants and the needs of those plants: proper light, heat, water, humidity, soil, and fertilizer. Also in the directory are some symptoms, causes, and cures for sick plants. The Plant Wheel, supplied separately and assembled in Activity 3, is used with Core Activities 3, 5, and 6. The wheel is used to aid students in identifying twelve common house plants and in learning the light and water requirements of those plants.

One advanced activity describes what happens inside a leaf cell during photosynthesis. The chemical reactions of photosynthesis are discussed. In another advanced activity, students study the effects of plant hormones called *auxins* on plant growth. And in a third advanced activity, students investigate the factors involved in the movement of water in a plant.

In the excursion activities, students make potting soil; repot, clean, and humidify house plants; use different methods to propagate house plants; and identify poor plant treatment and prescribe the correct treatment.

Plant Directory

The *Plant Directory* is a wall chart that should be positioned at eye level near a writing surface. The information in the directory is based on the information in *Plants Indoors*. For example, the propagation methods listed for each plant in the directory are those methods that are discussed in the minicourse. The fertilizer requirements given in the directory are for *established* plants as defined in the minicourse: plants that have been in potting soil for three to six months.

Plant Wheel

The Plant Wheel consists of a set of three spirit duplicating masters called *Plant Wheel, Cover; Plant Wheel, Circle;* and *Plant Wheel, Common House Plants.* Instructions for assembling the plant wheel are given in Activity 3.

Materials and Equipment

The following chart represents an estimate of needs based on "student units." The student unit may be one student working alone, two students working as partners, or several students working as a group. The size of the student unit will depend on the nature of the activity and on the availability of materials and equipment.

QUANTITY PER STUDENT UNIT	ITEMS	ACTIVITIES			NO. UNITS THAT CAN SHARE
		Core	Advanced	Excursion	
	Consumable				
200 ml	Alcohol, ethyl, 95% solution	8			
	Auxin paste		14		
1	Cardboard, lightweight 22 cm × 22 cm	3			
2	Cardboard, medium-weight 22 cm × 22 cm	3			
1	Celery stalk or coleus stem		15		
	Cellophane tape	3			
1	Crayon or colored pencil	8			
1 litre	Drainage materials (sand or perlite)			17	
8 ml	Fertilizer (5–10–5 or 12–6–6)			17	
10 drops	Food coloring		15		
1 litre	Garden soil (loam)			17	
	Glue	3			
40 ml	Iodine solution	8			
10 ml	Limestone, ground			17	
15 cm	Masking tape		14,15		
1 litre	Organic matter (peat moss or leaf mold)			17	
1	Paper fastener	3			
1	Pencil, grease	2	14	19	
2 copies	Plant Wheel, Circle	3			
2 copies	Plant Wheel, Cover	3			
1 copy	Plant Wheel, Common House Plants	3			
2–5	Plastic sheets or bags	2		19	
2–3 litres	Potting soil	2		18,19	
100 ml	Rooting medium	2		19	
about 0.5g	Rooting-hormone powder	2		19	
2 ml	Soap, for cleaning microscope slide		15		
5 ml	Superphosphate (20%)			17	
	Nonconsumable				
2	Beakers, 400 to 600-ml, heat-resistant	8			10
1	Bucket, with lid or large plastic bag with tie, 4 litres or larger			17	10
1	Glass capillary tube, 10 cm		15		10

Materials and Equipment (continued)

QUANTITY PER STUDENT UNIT	ITEMS	ACTIVITIES			NO. UNITS THAT CAN SHARE
		Core	Advanced	Excursion	
1	Glass stirring rod		14,15		5
5	Hair pins or 20 4-cm pieces of fine wire			19	10
1	Hot plate	8			10
2 or 3	House-plant fertilizer containers, empty or tightly closed	4			10
1	Jar, 1-litre		15		10
3	Jars, small (the size of baby food jars)	8	15		5
1	Knife, long bladed			18	10
1	Knife, sharp, or single-edged razor blade	2,8	15	19	3
1	Magnifying glass or hand lens		15		10
1	Measuring container, 1-litre			17	10
1	Measuring spoon, 5-ml			17	10
1	Medicine dropper		15		10
1	Microscope		13		10
1	Microscope slide		15		10
1	Pan, 6 cm deep	2		19	10
3	Petri dishes	8			10
1	*Plant Directory*	2,3,5, 6,7			5
1	Plant, healthy (coleus)	2,8	14	18	1
	†Plants, healthy			19	5
4	Pots, flower, small	2		18,19	1
1	Ruler, metric	2		19	5
1	Scissors	3			5
1	Scoop or spoon	2		18,19	5
1	Slide of leaf cross section		13		10
1	Spoon or mixing stick			17	10
3	Stakes, wooden, 20–30 cm	2		19	10
3	Stones, small or broken shards			18	5
5	Thermometers, Celsius	5			15
1	Tongs, beaker	8			10
1	Tweezers	8			10
1	*Resource Unit 3*		13		6
1	*Resource Unit 4*	10			6
1	*Resource Unit 12*		15		6
1	*Resource Unit 19*	10			6

†See Advance Preparation for Activity 19.

Activity 2 Core Page 6

In this activity stem cuttings are made. Students planning to do Activity 14 should make 3 stem cuttings and should begin Activity 14 immediately after doing this activity.

Potting soil is needed for this activity. If it is not available, students should make potting soil by doing Activity 17 before completing this activity. Also, clay or plastic pots are needed for this activity. Be sure to have a large supply available. Some students will need 3 pots or 1 large pot for 3 cuttings. For rooting hormone, any commercial brand may be used. (Rootone® is one such brand.)

Be sure to have available a storage area with adequate light for the students' cuttings.

Advance Preparation

Activity 3 Core Page 12

Be sure to make enough copies of the plant wheel materials. Each student needs 2 copies of *Plant Wheel, Cover;* 2 copies of *Plant Wheel, Circle;* and 1 copy of *Plant Wheel, Common House Plants.*

Medium-weight and lightweight pieces of cardboard (22 cm × 22 cm) are needed for the plant wheel. Suggestions for medium-weight cardboard are: the back of a pad of paper or the cardboard used by a laundry in shirts; suggestions for lightweight cardboard are: construction paper, a manila folder, or poster paper.

Activity 4 Core Page 16

Be sure to have available 2 or 3 different house-plant fertilizer containers that are empty or tightly closed. Students will examine the labels of these containers.

Activity 6 Core Page 24

If you set up a plant-watering experiment in the classroom, it will take about a week to prepare the plants. Recommended plants to use are coleus and aphelandra (zebra plant). Both plants are sensitive to overwatering and underwatering.

Use three mature plants, all about the same age and size. Overwater one plant. The effects of overwatering can be magnified by using a pot without a drainage hole. Keep the soil barely moist in another plant; and give just enough water to the third plant to keep it alive. You'll probably have to experiment to get the desired results. The effects should be obvious within a week.

Activity 7 Core Page 28

If possible, have sick plants available for students to diagnose and treat or to diagnose and write prescriptions for treatment. You may decide to make plants sick by providing inappropriate amounts of water, light, or heat. If you do this, be sure the plants get treated in time to prevent them from dying. If there are no sick plants available in the classroom, students may be able to bring some from home. But do not allow students to bring in plants that are infested with pests as you'll risk infesting your entire plant population.

Activity 8 Core Page 32

Two healthy coleus plants are needed for this activity. One plant is to be placed in the dark for at least 72 hours. The actual time needed for darkness may vary with the type of coleus plant used. So it's recommended that you do the investigation beforehand with the type of coleus your students will be using. Then, if necessary, adjust the period of time for which the plant must be kept in the dark.

After students remove a leaf from each plant, the plants can be returned to the light and used for other activities.

Preparation of iodine solution (100 ml): Lugol's solution can be prepared by dissolving 10 g of potassium iodide in 100 ml of distilled water. Then add 5 g of iodine crystals to the mixture. *Caution: iodine crystals are irritating to the skin. Be sure to handle with care.*

The solution should be stored in a dark, well-stoppered glass bottle and dispensed in a dropper bottle.

Activity 13 Advanced Page 50

If students want to make a crude leaf cross section before looking at the prepared slide, ask them to proceed as follows: Slice a length of raw carrot in half. Place a piece of leaf between the two carrot halves. With string or heavy thread, wrap the carrot halves together and soak in water for 3 or 4 hours. The carrot and the enclosed leaf will expand, becoming rigid enough to cut. With a sharp razor or hand microtome, slice thin sections at a slight angle. Keep both the razor blade and the tissue wet. Put the cut sections in water so they won't curl. Then mount each section in a drop of water.

Activity 14 Advanced Page 55

Each student needs 3 rooted coleus plants for this activity. Be sure to have plants available for students who need them. (The students who did Activity 2 should use the plants they rooted for that activity.)

The commercial form of auxin paste is usually 0.5% auxin. You may need to experiment with it to assure proper results in the allotted time.

You may get better results by making your own auxin paste. Proceed as follows: Put 10 g of anhydrous lanolin in a glass vial with a screw cap. Heat this in a water bath until the lanolin melts. Then add 0.1 g of indole-3-acetic acid (IAA) or 0.1 g of α-naphthaleneacetic acid. Stir well for several minutes. This makes a 1% auxin paste.

Activity 17 Excursion Page 66

The preparation of adequate potting soil depends on the type of loam available. In some areas the clay and/or sandy loam may be inadequate as a potting soil ingredient. In that case, it would be better to use commercial potting soil. Commercial potting soil and some of the other materials needed for this minicourse can be obtained from garden shops, discount department stores, supermarkets, or plant nurseries. If you use garden soil, it *must* be sterilized. See Excursion Page 67 for directions.

The potting soil ingredients may be measured with a 1-quart contrainer (about 1 litre) and a teaspoon (about 5 ml).

To store the potting soil and keep it moist, use a bucket covered with a tight-fitting lid or a plastic bag that's tied closed.

Activity 18 Excursion Page 68

Ideally, students should repot plants that actually need repotting, but the activity can be done with plants that don't need repotting.

One rooted plant is needed for each student doing this activity. If students do Activity 2, they can use the rooted plants from that activity. If they don't do Activity 2, rooted plants must be made available.

Potting soil is needed for this activity. Have some available or be sure that students do Activity 17 to mix their own soil. Also, each student needs a clay or plastic pot. Be sure the pots are available.

Activity 19 Excursion Page 73

One or more of the following mature plants are necessary for each cutting listed. Leaf cutting: African violet, gloxinia, peperomia, rex begonia. Leaf section cutting: rex begonia, wax begonia. Vein cutting: African violet, rex begonia.

Potting soil is needed for this activity. Have some available or be sure that students do Activity 17 to mix their own. For rooting hormone, any commercial brand may be used. (Rootone® is one such brand.)

Light Requirements

Background Information

In many plant and garden books, the light requirements of plants are specified in terms of foot-candles. A foot-candle is a unit in the English system of measurement for intensity of illumination. (In the International System of Units, a *candela* is the unit for intensity of illumination.)

A photographic light meter can be used to determine the light intensity that is available for a plant. First place a white card where the plant is to be located. Then set the light meter for ASA 100 and hold it near the white card. Adjust the dial to the needle so that they match. The inverse of the shutter speed reading at $f4$ will be the light intensity in foot-candles. Once you know the amount of light intensity available you can compare it to a plant's light requirement. This will tell whether your plants are getting enough light.

Figure 1 shows light requirements for some common plants.

Plant	Foot Candles
African violet (Saintpaulia)	400–1200
Areca palm (Chrysalidocarpus)	400+
Cacti (Cactaceae)	1000+
Coleus	400–1100
Dieffenbachia (Dumb cane)	100–500
Fern, Boston (Nephrolepis)	400+

Figure 1

Plant	Foot Candles
Geranium (Pelargonium)	1000–1500
Ivy (Hedera)	800–1300
Patient Lucy (Impatiens)	900–2200
Philodendron	20–1100
Rubber tree (Ficus)	400–1000
Sansevieria (Snake plant)	64–500
Aphelandra (Zebra plant)	1000–1500
Begonia, rex	500–1000
Begonia, wax	1000–1600
Dracaena	100–600
Gloxinia (Sinningia)	500–1500
Peperomia	500–1000
Poinsettia (Euphorbia)	1000–1500
Schefflera (Brassaia)	500–1100
Spider plant (Chlorophytum)	400+
Staghorn fern (Platycerium)	400+
Wandering Jew (Tradescantia and Zebrina)	400+

Figure 1

Essential Elements

If a plant's leaves turn yellow, it may be due to *chlorosis*. Chlorosis is a plant condition in which chlorophyll does not develop. This condition can be caused by a deficiency in any of the essential elements.

Some of the major elements needed by plants are nitrogen, phosphorus, and potassium. Nitrogen is a component of proteins, chlorophyll, amino acids, alkaloids, and plant hormones. Phosphorus is a component of some plant proteins and is vital for plant metabolism (ATP). The highest percentage of phosphorus is found in the areas of the plant that are growing rapidly. This is also true of potassium. Potassium seems to be critical for normal cell division, synthesis and translocation of carbohydrates, synthesis of proteins, development of chlorophyll, and movement of water.

A plant can't tell the difference between elements in synthetic fertilizers and elements in organic fertilizers. However, the breakdown of organic fertilizers provides organic acids which improve the porosity of the soil.

Overwatering

Two ways that overwatering causes plant deaths are:
1. Root hairs are essentially elongations of the epithelial cells of the root. They continuously develop, function for a few days, disintegrate naturally, and are replaced by new root hairs—

provided that the soil environment contains a balance of air and moisture. Periodic heavy watering is good for the soil environment because it replaces the water that has drained out and the water used by the plant. But continuous heavy watering prevents the soil from having a balance of water and air. Thus, the oxygen supply becomes limited and the root cells can't carry on respiration. The roots are deprived of energy and eventually the plant dies.

2. The soil must be porous enough to permit the movement of air which brings in oxygen to the plant and removes carbon dioxide. Continuous overwatering causes the soil to become less porous. Then carbon dioxide accumulates; the soil becomes toxic; root action decreases; and the plant may die.

Evaluation Suggestions

In addition to the Minicourse Test, you might use some or all of the essay questions and laboratory experiences to evaluate your students.

Essay Questions

Two essay questions and their possible answers follow. Both questions are related to core material.

1. Suppose a friend has a large coleus plant and has given you permission to make a stem cutting. Describe what you'd do to root the cutting. Be sure to include all the steps.

Answer: a. Prepare a pot with moist potting soil. Dig a small hole in the soil and fill the hole with rooting medium.
b. Find a stem with new growth and make a diagonal cut just below a leaf joint.
c. Remove any leaves from the bottom part of the stem and dip the stem into rooting hormone.
d. Push the stem into the rooting medium in the pot. Sprinkle some water on the leaves, push 2 or 3 stakes into the soil, and cover the plant with plastic. (Don't let the plastic touch the plant's leaves.)
e. Store in a well-lighted place, but not in direct sunlight. When new leaves appear, the plant will be rooted.

2. Describe the processes of photosynthesis and respiration in plants. Explain why respiration can take place in the presence or absence of light and why photosynthesis can take place only in the presence of light.

Answer: Photosynthesis is a process during which water and carbon dioxide are combined to form glucose. For photosynthesis to occur, plants need light and chlorophyll.

Respiration is the process by which green plants get energy from food. During respiration, the starch in the plant's cells is changed to glucose which is then combined with oxygen from the air. Carbon dioxide and water are produced and energy is provided to the plant.

Plants need energy all the time. They are constantly getting energy from food. Hence in both the presence and absence of light, respiration takes place. Light energy is needed for photosynthesis to occur. When there's no light, photosynthesis cannot take place.

Laboratory Performance

1. Ask students to demonstrate the proper technique for transplanting or repotting a plant.

2. Obtain a sick house plant that is ailing because of lack of light, water, or fertilizer. Ask students to diagnose the problem and to prescribe treatment.

3. Give students a copy of *Plant Wheel, Common House Plants.* Ask them to identify some or all of the plant sketches.

4. Give students a live plant, photograph, or sketch of one or more common house plants that appear in the plant wheel. Choose types of plants that were not used for the investigations in *Plants Indoors.* Ask students to identify each plant and also to state its light and water requirements.

Bechtel, H. 1973. *House plant identifier.* New York: Sterling Publishing Company.

This is an excellent, inexpensive plant encyclopedia of 120 common house plants. The book has attractive colored photographs and important information on the care of the plants that are listed.

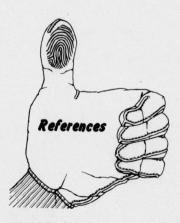

References

Crockett, J. U. 1971. *Flowering house plants.* The Time-Life Encyclopedia of Gardening. New York: Time-Life Books.

This highly readable book presents the techniques for the proper care of flowering house plants. It contains an encyclopedic chapter which lists the characteristics and needs of 145 genera of flowering house plants.

_____. 1971. *Foliage house plants.* The Time-Life Encyclopedia of Gardening. New York: Time-Life Books.

This book describes the proper techniques for the care and maintenance of foliage plants. An encyclopedic chapter lists the growing requirements, as well as the characteristics, uses, and methods of propagating 103 genera of foliage house plants.

Govindjee, and Govindjee, Rajni. 1974. The absorption of light in photosynthesis. *Scientific American.* 231: 68–82 D.

This is a technical treatment of the initial processes of photosynthesis in which light is absorbed by a specific molecule, and energy is transferred from one molecule to another. This article is most suitable as a reference for teachers and for students doing Advanced Activity 13, *Inside the Photosynthesis Factory.*

Morholt, E.; Brandwein, P. F.; and Joseph, A. 1966. *A sourcebook for the biological sciences.* 2nd ed. New York: Harcourt Brace Jovanovich, Inc.

This is an excellent manual for every biology laboratory. Chapters 9 and 13 provide a wealth of information on the growth of plants and experimenting with plants in the laboratory. Chapter 3 has an in-depth treatment of the photosynthesis process.

Sunset Editors. 1968. *How to grow house plants.* Menlo Park, California: Lane Magazine and Book Company.

This is a highly pictorialized treatment of flowering and foliage plants. It includes both indoor and outdoor plants. Special features are bottle and miniature gardens as well as terrariums.

The following booklet is available at low cost from the U.S. Department of Agriculture. It can be obtained in class-size quantities from the Superintendent of Documents, U.S. Government Printing Office, Washington, D.C. 20401

Selecting and Growing House Plants

This 32-page booket gives the description, culture, and special requirements of many foliage and flowering house plants.

ISIS

INDIVIDUALIZED SCIENCE INSTRUCTIONAL SYSTEM

PLANTS INDOORS

Ginn and Company

A XEROX EDUCATION COMPANY

Acknowledgments

In addition to the major effort by the ISIS permanent staff, writing conference participants, and author-consultants (listed on the inside back cover), the following contributed to this minicourse.

Art created by: Brian Cody; Frank Fretz; David Kingham.

Design and production supplied by: Kirchoff/Wohlberg, Inc.

Cover designed by: Martucci Studio

Reviewers: James J. Franklin, Associate Professor of Horticulture, Rural Development Division, School of Science and Technology, Florida Agricultural and Mechanical University, Tallahassee, Florida; Dr. Peter H. Homann, Associate Professor of Biological Science, Florida State University, Tallahassee, Florida.

The work presented or reported herein was supported by a grant from the National Science Foundation. However, the opinions expressed herein do not necessarily reflect the position or policy of the National Science Foundation, and no official endorsement by that agency should be inferred.

Ginn and Company
A Xerox Education Company
Home Office: Lexington, Massachusetts 02173
0-663-33766-6
0-663-33626-0

FOREWORD

Evidence has been mounting that something is missing from secondary science teaching. More and more, students are rejecting science courses and turning to subjects that they consider to be more practical or significant. Numerous high school science teachers have concluded that what they are now teaching is appropriate for only a limited number of their students.

As their concern has mounted, many science teachers have tried to find instructional materials that encompass more appropriate content and that allow them to work individually with students who have different needs and talents. For the most part, this search has been frustrating because presently such materials are difficult, if not impossible, to find.

The Individualized Science Instructional System (ISIS) project was organized to produce an alternative for those teachers who are dissatisfied with current secondary science textbooks. Consequently, the content of the ISIS materials is unconventional as is the individualized teaching method that is built into them. In contrast with many current science texts which aim to "cover science," ISIS has tried to be selective and to limit our coverage to the topics that we judge will be most useful to today's students.

Obviously the needs and problems of individual schools and students vary widely. To accommodate the differences, ISIS decided against producing tightly structured, pre-sequenced textbooks. Instead, we are generating short, self-contained modules that cover a wide range of topics. The modules can be clustered into many types of courses, and we hope that teachers and administrators will utilize this flexibility to tailor-make curricula that are responsive to local needs and conditions.

ISIS is a cooperative effort involving many individuals and agencies. More than 75 scientists and educators have helped to generate the materials, and hundreds of teachers and thousands of students have been involved in the project's nationwide testing program. All of the ISIS endeavors have been supported by generous grants from the National Science Foundation. We hope that ISIS users will conclude that these large investments of time, money, and effort have been worthwhile.

Ernest Burkman
ISIS Project
Tallahassee, Florida

CONTENTS

What's It All About?   1

CORE ACTIVITIES
Activity 1: Planning   2
Activity 2: Propagating House Plants   6
Activity 3: Identifying House Plants   12
Activity 4: Fertilizer Facts   16
Activity 5: Where Plants Grow Best   20
Activity 6: Watering Properly   24
Activity 7: Plant Problems   28
Activity 8: Photosynthesis and Respiration   32
Activity 9: Plant Growth Experiments   39
Activity 10: What's Normal?   43
Activity 11: Greening a Room (Required)   46

ADVANCED ACTIVITIES
Activity 12: Planning   48
Activity 13: Inside the Photosynthesis Factory   50
Activity 14: Plant Hormones   55
Activity 15: Plant Plumbing   59

EXCURSION ACTIVITIES
Activity 16: Planning   65
Activity 17: Make Your Own Potting Soil   66
Activity 18: Potpourri   68
Activity 19: More On Propagation   73
Activity 20: Plant Blunders   76

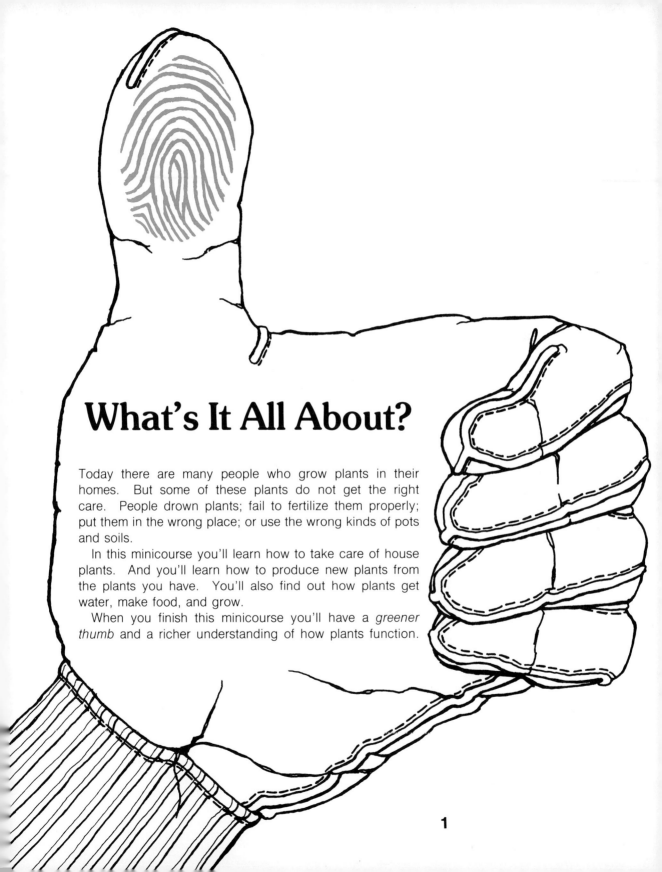

What's It All About?

Today there are many people who grow plants in their homes. But some of these plants do not get the right care. People drown plants; fail to fertilize them properly; put them in the wrong place; or use the wrong kinds of pots and soils.

In this minicourse you'll learn how to take care of house plants. And you'll learn how to produce new plants from the plants you have. You'll also find out how plants get water, make food, and grow.

When you finish this minicourse you'll have a *greener thumb* and a richer understanding of how plants function.

1

core

Activity **1** Planning

This minicourse requires some careful planning. Follow these directions for the activities you need to do:

Do Activity 2 first.

Do Activity 3 before doing Activity 5 or 6.

Do Activity 11 last. It is a required activity.

Activity **2** Page 6

Objective 1: Identify and briefly describe three methods for propagating house plants.

Sample Question: Match each propagating method in List A with the description in List B.

List A

1. layering

2. division

3. cuttings

List B

a. separating stems that have one root system

b. getting roots to grow from a stem which is connected to the parent plant

c. getting roots to grow from a piece of a stem or leaf

Activity **3** Page 12

Objective 2: Identify twelve common house plants using sketches, photographs, or live plants.

Sample Question: Name the plants shown in Figure 1–1.

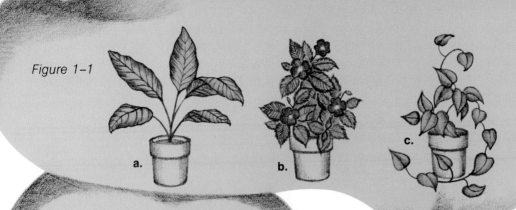

Figure 1–1

a.

b.

c.

Activity 4 Page 16

Objective 3: Name the three essential elements that plants get from fertilizer.

Sample Question: What three essential elements do plants get from fertilizer?

Objective 4: Tell how to properly fertilize house plants.

Sample Question: Before you fertilize a plant, the soil should be:
a. very wet.
b. moist.
c. dry.

Activity 5 Page 20

Objective 5: Identify the light requirements of twelve common house plants.

Sample Question: Match each plant in List A with its light requirement from List B.

List A
1. geranium
2. philodendron
3. cactus
List B
a. dim light
b. filtered or indirect light
c. bright sunlight

Activity 6 Page 24

Objective 6: Name the water requirements for twelve common house plants.

Sample Question: Which statement is true for the soil of a coleus plant?
a. Keep the soil wet.
b. Keep the soil slightly moist.
c. Let the soil dry out.

Objective 7: Describe three ways to properly water house plants.

Sample Question: Which rule should you follow when watering a potted plant from the top?
a. Use cold water.
b. Gently spray the water on the leaves.
c. Add water until it comes out the drain hole.

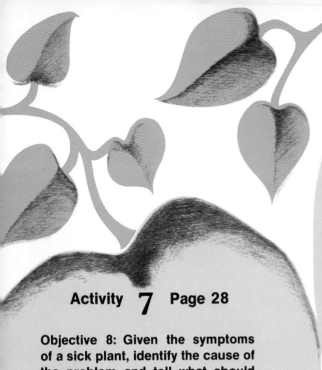

Activity 7 Page 28

Objective 8: Given the symptoms of a sick plant, identify the cause of the problem and tell what should be done.

Sample Question: What might cause a plant to have these symptoms: dark, mushy stems; yellow, wilted lower leaves; green scum on the outside of its clay pot?
a. too much water
b. too much fertilizer
c. mealy bugs

Objective 9: Identify insecticides suitable for use on house plants and tell how to safely use the insecticides.

Sample Question: Which insecticide is suitable for use on house plants?
a. DDT
b. malathion
c. chlordane

Activity 8 Page 32

Objective 10: Describe the processes of photosynthesis and respiration in plants.

Sample Question: Which statement is true for photosynthesis?
a. Energy is produced from food.
b. Light is used to produce food.
c. Carbon dioxide is used to make chlorophyll.

Objective 11: Explain why photosynthesis is important to all living things.

Sample Question: Why is photosynthesis important to all living things?
a. All living things use the photosynthesis process to make food.
b. Living things need the carbon dioxide and oxygen produced by photosynthesis.
c. Living things need the stored energy produced by photosynthesis.

Activity 9 Page 39

Objective 12: Identify which conclusions from plant growth experiments are *not* supported by observations.

Sample Question: A student did an experiment with grass seedlings (see Figure 1–2). Then the student made the following three conclusions based on the experiment:
a. Light influences a normal shoot to bend.
b. A substance produced in the tip of the shoot causes the bending.
c. Somehow the plastic causes the shoot not to bend.
Which conclusions are not supported by the experiment?

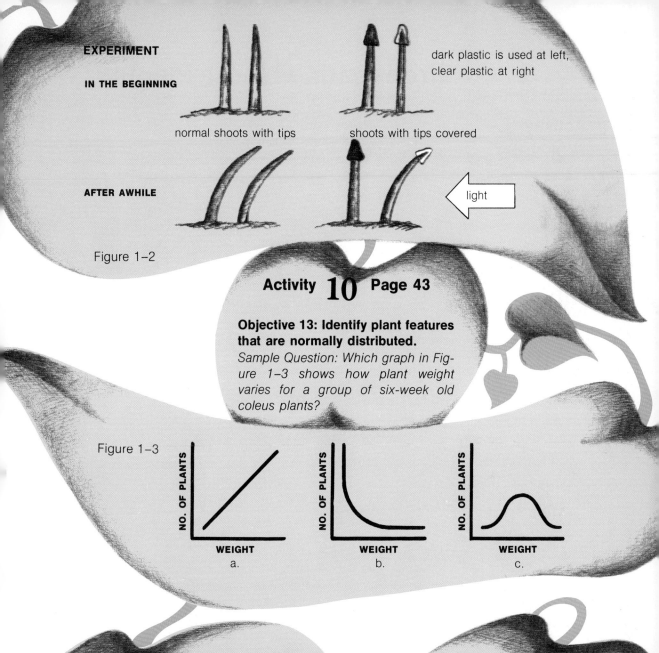

EXPERIMENT

IN THE BEGINNING

dark plastic is used at left, clear plastic at right

normal shoots with tips

shoots with tips covered

AFTER AWHILE

light

Figure 1–2

Activity 10 Page 43

Objective 13: Identify plant features that are normally distributed.

Sample Question: Which graph in Figure 1–3 shows how plant weight varies for a group of six-week old coleus plants?

Figure 1–3

a.
NO. OF PLANTS / WEIGHT

b.
NO. OF PLANTS / WEIGHT

c.
NO. OF PLANTS / WEIGHT

Activity 11 Page 46

REQUIRED
In this activity you'll use plants to decorate a room.

Answers
1. 1-b, 2-a, 3-c 2. a. Dieffenbachia (dumb cane) b.Impatiens (patient Lucy) c. Philodendron 3. Nitrogen (N), Phosphorus (P), Potassium (K) 4. b
5. 1-c, 2-b, 3-b or 3-c 6. b 7. c 8. a
9. b 10. b 11. c 12. b and c 13. c

Propagating House Plants

ACTIVITY EMPHASIS: Described in this activity are three methods for propagating house plants. Students investigate one of these methods, *cuttings*, by making stem cuttings.

Suppose you wanted to decorate a room with house plants.

You could buy the plants. Garden and flower shops sell many different plants. This is the easy way. And it is sometimes an expensive way.

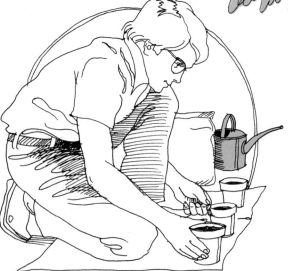

You could grow new plants from seeds. The seeds may be bought at a store or taken directly from a plant. Propagating or reproducing plants from seeds can be interesting and fun.

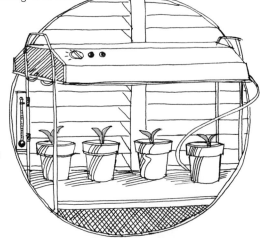

But most of these plants grow slowly and need special conditions.

6   CORE

As you can see, there are problems involved with propagating (reproducing) plants from seeds. But there are ways to propagate plants without seeds.

Plants have two ways of reproducing. One way is by sexual reproduction: The sperm of the pollen joins with the eggs of the flower. Seeds are formed. Humans and other higher forms of animals, as well as plants, reproduce sexually.

Plants can also reproduce asexually. This method is called *vegetative propagation*. Instead of a seed, a piece of plant is used. It develops into a new plant.

✔ 2–1. The first *a* in asexual means *not*. Why is vegetative propagation *not* sexual reproduction? 2-1. Because the sperm and the egg do not unite to form a seed.

There are several advantages to vegetative propagation. One advantage is that the new plants are exactly like the parent plant.

✔ 2–2. Explain why the new plants are exactly like the parent plant. 2-2. A new plant has the same genes as the parent plant; it looks exactly like the parent plant.

Another advantage of vegetative propagation is that you, the grower, can select the plants you want to propagate. When you choose a healthy parent, the new plants will also be healthy. And the new plants will grow and mature faster than plants started from seeds.

The three general techniques for vegetative propagation are *division, cuttings, and layering.* The most common methods for these techniques are shown in Figure 2–1, pages 7, 8, and 9. Also shown is a rating for each method: from difficult to easy. And there is a list of plants· for which each method works. The *Plant Directory* will help you identify the plants.

MATERIALS PER STUDENT UNIT
spoon or scoop
small pot for each cutting or large pot for 3 cuttings
potting soil
metric ruler
rooting medium[1]
mature plant[2]
rooting-hormone powder[3]
single-edged razor blade or sharp knife
2-3 wooden stakes, 20-30 cm[4]
clear plastic sheet or bag
small pan, 6 cm deep
grease pencil
water
Plant Directory
1. Can be coarse sand, perlite, sphagnum moss, vermiculite, or any two of these in a 1:1 combination. If the rooting medium is not sterile, bake it at 82°C (180°F) for 30 minutes. This will prevent fungus growth.
2. Coleus is recommended. Otherwise, use ivy or philodendron. Plant should be mature enough to have several well-developed branches. Then cuttings may be made without injury to the plant.
3. Rootone® or other commercial products are satisfactory. *Caution:* Too much rooting hormone sometimes causes rotting of herbacious plant stems.
4. Bent wire coat hangers may be used instead of the stakes.

COMMON METHODS OF VEGETATIVE PROPAGATION

DIVISION	
Less Easy	Plants: aluminum plant, most ferns, peperomia, sansevieria, spider plant

If students do not know much about genetics, they may not be able to answer
Figure 2–1 Question 2-2. The answer is not critical to the activity.

bent hangers

CORE 7

CUTTINGS Stem Cuttings Easy	Plants: azalea, some cacti, chrysanthemum, coleus, dieffenbachia, gardenia, geranium, holly, ivy, jade, patient Lucy, philodendron, succulents, most vines	
Leaf Cuttings Less Easy	Plants: African violet, gloxinia, peperomia, rex begonia	
Leaf Section Cuttings Less Easy	Plants: sansevieria, rex begonia, wax begonia	
Vein Cuttings Difficult	Plants: African violet, rex begonia	

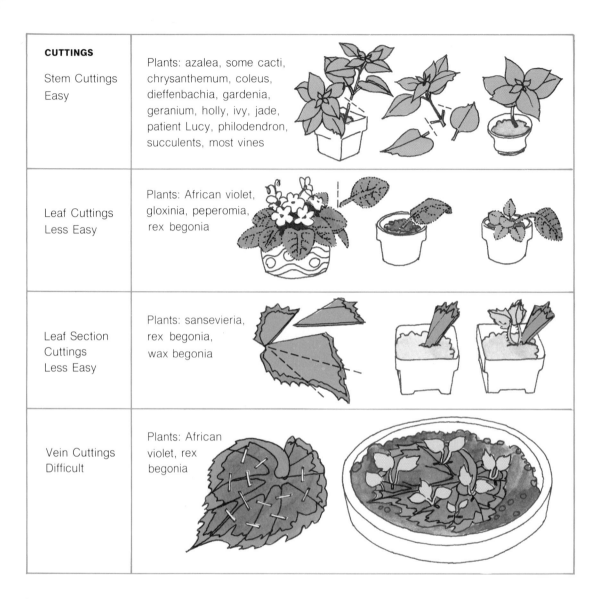

LAYERING Soil Layering (Rooting Runners) Easy	Plants: ivy, spider plant, strawberry geranium, vining philodendron

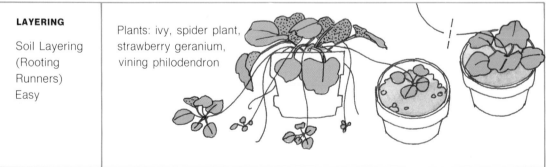

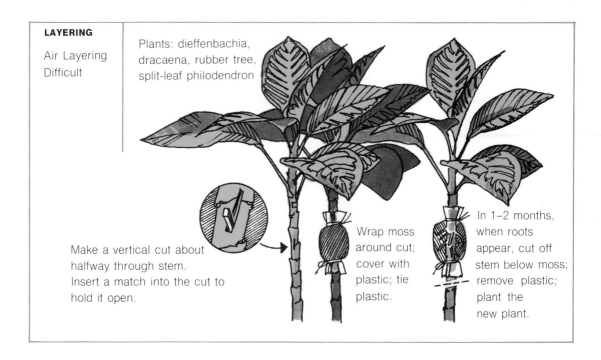

LAYERING

Air Layering
Difficult

Plants: dieffenbachia, dracaena, rubber tree, split-leaf philodendron

Make a vertical cut about halfway through stem. Insert a match into the cut to hold it open.

Wrap moss around cut; cover with plastic; tie plastic.

In 1–2 months, when roots appear, cut off stem below moss; remove plastic; plant the new plant.

✔ 2–3. In layering, the new plant's roots grow from which part of the parent plant?

★ **2–4. How is division different from layering?**

In this activity, you'll make a stem cutting. Later you'll use the cutting in Activity 14 or 18. In fact you'll use *three* cuttings in Activity 14. So turn to *Activity 12: Planning* to see if you can do what is stated in the objectives for Activity 14.

If you plan to do Activity 14, make three stem cuttings. If not, make one cutting. You'll need about 45 minutes for this investigation. Get the following materials for each cutting:

grease pencil for labeling
pot
* potting soil
spoon or scoop for potting
    soil
metric ruler
small pan
water

rooting medium
mature plant, to take
    cutting from
sharp knife
rooting-hormone powder
2 or 3 stakes
sheet of clear plastic or
    a clear plastic bag

* If potting soil is not available, you'll have to prepare your own. Turn to Activity 17 for instructions.

2-3. From the stem of the parent plant.

2-4. In division, the parent plant is separated into 2 or more plants, each having the stems and roots of the parent plant. In layering, new roots must be grown for the new plant.

Note the directions in the text for students planning to do the advanced activities. Be sure students follow these directions.

In vegetative propagation the new plants should be kept moist—but they should not be drowned. So before making a stem cutting, you must get the right moisture for your plant.

A. Label the pot and fill it with potting soil. Then place the pot in a pan of water. Let the soil soak for *15 minutes.* While you're waiting, go to another activity.

soil 1 cm from top of pot

water

B. Pour the water from the pan and let the soil drain for *15 minutes.* Go to another activity while you're waiting. When the soil has drained, dig a hole in it. Fill the hole with rooting medium.

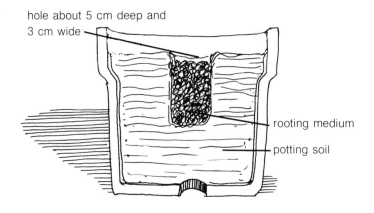

hole about 5 cm deep and 3 cm wide

rooting medium

potting soil

C. Get the plant and find a stem with a new growth. Make a diagonal cut about 10 cm from the tip of the stem and just below a leaf joint.

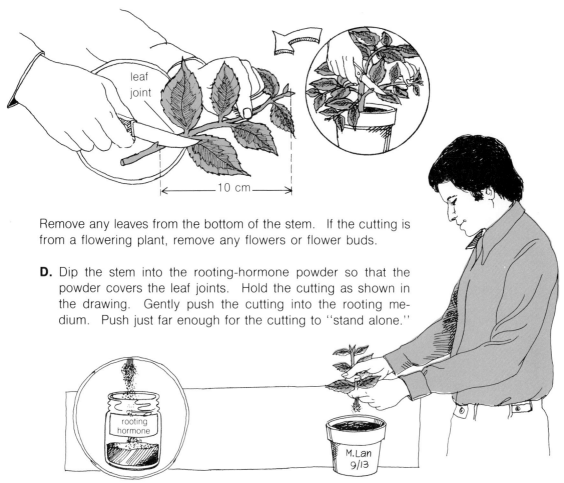

Remove any leaves from the bottom of the stem. If the cutting is from a flowering plant, remove any flowers or flower buds.

D. Dip the stem into the rooting-hormone powder so that the powder covers the leaf joints. Hold the cutting as shown in the drawing. Gently push the cutting into the rooting medium. Push just far enough for the cutting to "stand alone."

E. Push the stakes into the soil until they hit the bottom of the pot. Sprinkle a little water on the plant's leaves. Then place the plastic over the stakes and tuck it under the pot. The plastic must not touch the plant.

The plant should stay moist. But if it seems to be wilting, remove the plastic and resoak the pot. Be sure to replace the plastic.

✔ 2–5. How does the plastic cover help to keep the plant moist? 2-5. Water can't evaporate through the plastic, so the plant stays moist.

✔ 2–6. Why is a clear, colorless piece of plastic used?
2-6. It allows the plant to get plenty of light.

CORE 11

2-7. *a.* Prepare the potting soil: soak and drain the soil; dig a hole in it; fill the hole with rooting medium.

   b. From the parent plant, cut a stem with new growth. Remove any leaves from the bottom of the stem and any flowers or flower buds.

   c. Dip the end of the stem into rooting hormone. Insert the stem into the rooting medium in the potting soil.

   d. Sprinkle water on the leaves; push stakes into the soil; cover the plant and pot with plastic. Don't let the plastic touch the plant's leaves.

   e. Place the plant in well-lighted area. Uncover it when new growth appears.

Remind students to save the cuttings for use in Activities 14 and 18.

Store the plant in a well-lighted place, but not in direct sunlight. Then go to another activity. Be sure to check the plant every couple of days. When new leaves appear, the plant will be rooted.

Loosen the plastic but leave it draped over the sticks for a few days. This helps the plant adjust to the air and room temperature. Then remove the plastic. The plant should continue to grow well.

★ **2–7. Describe the 4 or 5 basic steps in growing a new plant from a stem cutting.**

If you plan to do Activity 14 in the advanced activities, do it now. You'll use the three cuttings from this activity. Then come back to the core activities.

If you plan to do the excursion activities, look at Activities 18 and 19. If you're interested in doing Activity 18, you'll use the cutting from this activity. So, until you do Activity 18, keep the cutting in a well-lighted area and be sure to water it.

Activity 19 shows other techniques for starting a plant. If you're interested in doing Activity 19, do it now. Then come back to the core activities.

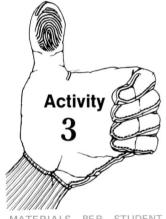

Activity 3

MATERIALS PER STUDENT UNIT
2 copies *Plant Wheel, Cover*
2 copies *Plant Wheel, Circle*
1 copy *Plant Wheel, Common House Plants*
scissors
paper fastener
2 pieces cardboard, medium-weight, 22 cm X 22 cm
1 piece cardboard, lightweight, 22 cm X 22 cm
glue
cellophane tape
Plant Directory

ACTIVITY EMPHASIS: Students make a plant wheel and use it to help identify twelve common house plants.

Identifying House Plants

Hey, what kind of plant is this? Sometimes this is a hard question to answer. But you should be able to identify some of the most common house plants. In this activity you'll make a plant wheel to help you identify plants. You'll need these materials:

2 copies of *Plant Wheel, Cover*
2 copies of *Plant Wheel, Circle*
scissors
2 pieces of cardboard, medium-weight, about 22 cm × 22 cm
1 piece of cardboard, lightweight, about 22 cm × 22 cm
glue
cellophane tape
1 copy of *Plant Wheel, Common House Plants*
Plant Directory
paper fastener

For suggestions on types of cardboard to use for the plant wheel, see Advanced Preparation, page TM 7.

12 CORE

A. Glue a plant wheel cover to a piece of medium-weight cardboard. Cut along the solid line of the cover. Be sure to cut both the paper and the cardboard. Do the same thing for the other plant wheel cover.

B. Glue a plant wheel circle to a piece of lightweight cardboard. Cut along the line forming the largest circle. Be sure to cut both the paper and the cardboard.

 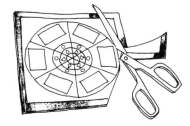

C. Cut out the other plant wheel circle. (Do *not* glue it to cardboard before cutting it.) Remember to cut along the line forming the largest circle. Then glue this circle to the other side of the cardboard from Step B.

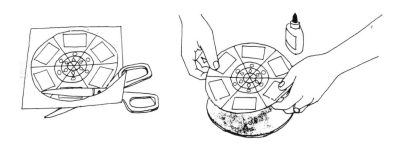

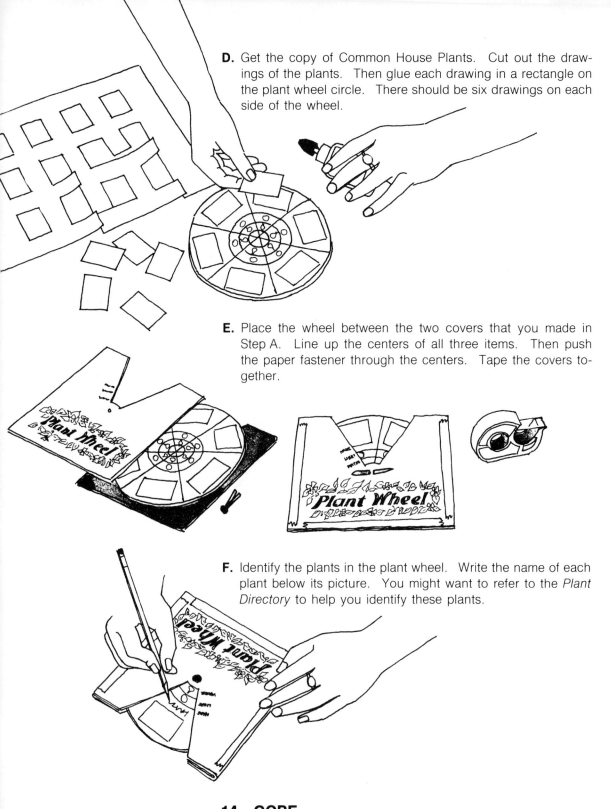

D. Get the copy of Common House Plants. Cut out the draw-ings of the plants. Then glue each drawing in a rectangle on the plant wheel circle. There should be six drawings on each side of the wheel.

E. Place the wheel between the two covers that you made in Step A. Line up the centers of all three items. Then push the paper fastener through the centers. Tape the covers to-gether.

F. Identify the plants in the plant wheel. Write the name of each plant below its picture. You might want to refer to the *Plant Directory* to help you identify these plants.

Study the plant wheel until you can identify each plant. Then look at the first twelve plants in the *Plant Directory*. These are the plants in your plant wheel but the pictures are different. Try to identify each plant without looking at its name. When you can do this, find a partner who is also doing this activity. Test each other's ability to identify the plants.

Do all the same type of plants look exactly alike? No, neither do all people look exactly alike. Questions 3–1 through 3–6 should help you identify plants that have common features. Use your plant wheel to answer the questions.

Encourage students to find live house plants to identify. These might be found in other classrooms, at home, or where house plants may be purchased.

3-1. *African violet* — hairy, rounded leaves; flowers in clusters. *Geranium* — horseshoe-shaped leaves; flowers in large clusters. *Patient Lucy* — pointed leaves; flowers in small clusters.

✔ 3–1. Name the plants that have flowers. How do these plants differ from each other?

✔ 3–2. Name the plants that do not have leaves. Describe what these plants look like. 3-2. Cacti — Fleshy shapes with spines.

✔ 3–3. Name the plants with leaves that are more than one shade or color. How do these plants differ from each other?

✔ 3–4. Name the plants that have a central stem (one main stem). How do these plants differ from each other?

✔ 3–5. Name the plants that are vines. How do these plants differ from each other? 3-5. *Ivy* — see answer for 3-3. *Philodendron* — see answer for 3-4.

✔ 3–6. Name the plants that do not have a central stem (one main stem). How do these plants differ from each other?
3-6. *African violet* — see answer for 3-1. *Cacti* — see answer for 3-2. *Boston fern* — sword-shaped fronds with tiny leaflets. *Sansevieria* — see answer for 3-3.

3-3. *Coleus* — one or two colors radiating from center of the leaves, and/or speckled markings throughout leaves. *Dieffenbachia* — speckled green-and-white markings or vein stripes on leaves. *Geranium* — wide bands around green horseshoe-shaped leaves. The bands are white or shades of green. *Ivy* — some varieties have leaf markings that are white or shades of green. The leaves grow on a vine and have lobes. *Sansevieria* — light zigzag stripes on leaves.

3-4. *Areca palm* — long fronds with thin leaflets. *Coleus* — see answer for 3-3. *Dieffenbachia* — see answer for 3-3. *Geranium* — see answer for 3-3. *Ivy* — see answer for 3-3. *Patient Lucy* — see answer for 3-1. *Philodendron* — heart-shaped leaves on vine or large leaves with lobes. *Rubber tree* — dark green, oval leaves.

CORE 15

Now identify each plant in Questions 3–7 to 3–12. If there are plants in your classroom, try to identify them too.

★ 3-7. VINE?

★ 3-8. STEM?

★ 3-9. COLOR?

★ 3-10. STEM?

★ 3-11. LEAVES?

★ 3-12. LEAVES?

3-7. Ivy.   3-8. Sansevieria.   3-9. Coleus.   3-10. Rubber tree.   3-11. Cactus.   3-12. Areca palm.

Keep your plant wheel. You'll need it later for Activities 5 and 6.

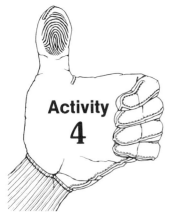

Activity 4

MATERIALS PER STUDENT UNIT
2 or 3 different house-plant fertilizer containers, empty or tightly closed.

ACTIVITY EMPHASIS: Presented in this activity are three essential mineral elements that plants obtain from fertilizers and some helpful hints for properly using fertilizers.

Fertilizer Facts

What makes a plant healthy and happy? Does a plant need more than light, air, water, and tender loving care? Scientists have identified sixteen chemical elements that plants need in order to live and grow. These elements are listed in Figure 4–1. The major elements are needed in relatively large amounts. The trace elements are needed in smaller amounts. The chemical symbol for each element is shown.

16 CORE

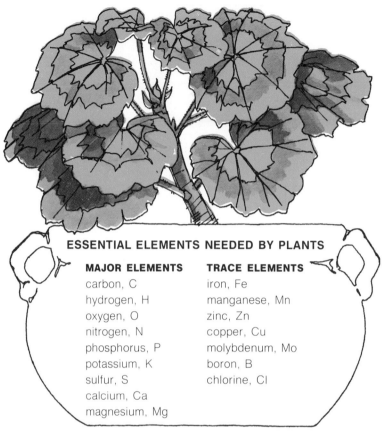

ESSENTIAL ELEMENTS NEEDED BY PLANTS

MAJOR ELEMENTS	TRACE ELEMENTS
carbon, C	iron, Fe
hydrogen, H	manganese, Mn
oxygen, O	zinc, Zn
nitrogen, N	copper, Cu
phosphorus, P	molybdenum, Mo
potassium, K	boron, B
sulfur, S	chlorine, Cl
calcium, Ca	
magnesium, Mg	

Figure 4–1

✔ 4–1. What major elements do plants get from water (H_2O) and carbon dioxide (CO_2)?

4-1. Hydrogen and oxygen from water; carbon and oxygen from carbon dioxide.

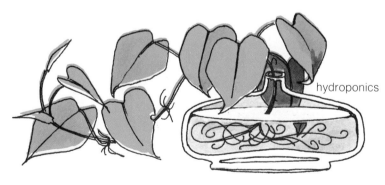

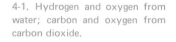

hydroponics

Other essential elements that a plant needs must come from the soil, through the plant's roots. When plants are grown in water, the water must supply the essential elements.

Suppose. . . Someone gives you a house plant. It needs a new pot.

You go outside and get some dirt.

For a while the plant grows all right in the soil.

Then the lower leaves turn yellow and die. The new leaves are small. The plant seems to stop growing.

What's wrong with the plant in the drawing? Probably some of the major essential elements have been used up. Fertilizer or plant food will provide these major elements: nitrogen, phosphorus, and potassium. Nitrogen and phosphorus atoms are in most of the molecules in a plant. Potassium helps control many of the processes that go on in plants

NITROGEN	PHOSPHORUS	POTASSIUM
Nitrogen is provided in fertilizer in the form of *nitrate,* *urea,* or *ammonia.*	Phosphorus is provided in fertilizer in the form of available *phosphoric acid.*	Potassium is provided in fertilizer in the form of *potash.*

A shortage of any of these elements is bad for a plant. But it's very difficult to relate a given symptom to a shortage of a certain element. Proper fertilizing is the key to keeping plants healthy.

If your plants were recently potted in good potting soil, you won't have to fertilize them for three to six months. When you do fertilize them, follow this procedure.

FERTILIZING HOUSE PLANTS

1 Read the directions on the container. Don't use more than the recommended amount of fertilizer. Too much fertilizer can kill a plant.

2 Consult the *Plant Directory* or another resource. Find out how often to fertilize each type of plant.

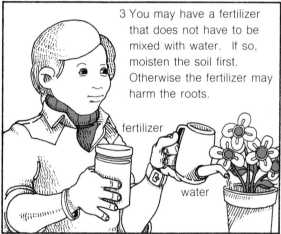

3 You may have a fertilizer that does not have to be mixed with water. If so, moisten the soil first. Otherwise the fertilizer may harm the roots.

fertilizer

water

4 Feed plants only when they are growing and can use the elements. Don't feed plants that are not growing, sick plants, or recently repotted plants.

HEALTHY YES

SICK OR NOT GROWING

NO

✔ 4–2. Cactus plants are dormant in the winter. Should they be fertilized in the winter? Explain.

★ **4–3. What are the steps to follow when fertilizing house plants?**

Read the labels on two or three containers of different house-plant fertilizers. Then answer Questions 4–4 and 4–5.

★ **4–4. What essential elements do the fertilizers supply?**

✔ 4–5. Describe any differences in the application methods.

4-2. No. Dormant plants are not growing and can't use fertilizer.

4-3. a. Follow the directions on the package.
  b. Know how much and how often to fertilize plants.
  c. Before applying fertilizer, mix it with water or moisten the soil.

4-4. Nitrogen, Phosphorus, and Potassium.

4-5. Answers will depend on the types of fertilizers that are available.

Percentages of essential elements are often listed on each container. They are usually listed as shown below.

nitrate : phosphoric acid : potash

A commercial fertilizer for foliage plants is likely to have the ratio 1:2:1. This may be written in equivalent forms such as 5:10:5 or 10:20:10. Notice that the middle number is the greatest number. This means that the percentage of phosphoric acid is greater than the percentage of nitrate or potash. The larger the numbers in the ratio, the more care must be taken in applying the fertilizer.

4-6. The ratio means that this fertilizer provides 10% nitrate, 10% phosphoric acid, and 20% potash.

✔ 4-6. Suppose 10:10:20 is the ratio shown for a fertilizer. What does this ratio mean?

ACTIVITY EMPHASIS: Students investigate the temperature and light conditions of various locations in a room. Then they match the temperature and light requirements of plants in the plant wheel with corresponding conditions in the room.

Where Plants Grow Best

Activity 5

Plants won't grow just anywhere. Each kind of plant needs the right conditions of light and temperature. So you must be careful about where you put plants.

In this activity you'll study the effects of different temperatures and amounts of light on plants. Then you'll decide which plants grow best in certain places in your classroom or home. You'll need these materials:

5 Celsius thermometers
plant wheel from Activity 3 or a list consisting of the first 12 plants in the *Plant Directory*
Plant Directory

A. Find a place in your classroom or home that's like each location illustrated. Then draw a chart like the one in Figure 5-1. In the first column, describe each location you found. For example, one description might be *the table next to the southwest window*.

MATERIALS PER STUDENT UNIT
5 Celsius thermometers[1]
Plant Directory
Plant wheel from Activity 3, or plant list[2]

1. Small, inexpensive thermometers will suffice.

2. If students do not have a plant wheel, and you want them to make one, ask them to do the investigation in Activity 3.

LOCATIONS

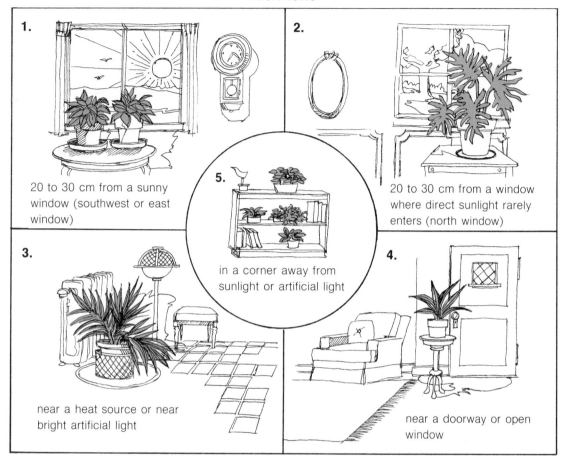

1. 20 to 30 cm from a sunny window (southwest or east window)

2. 20 to 30 cm from a window where direct sunlight rarely enters (north window)

3. near a heat source or near bright artificial light

4. near a doorway or open window

5. in a corner away from sunlight or artificial light

PLANTS AND THEIR ENVIRONMENT

LOCATION	TEMP. DAY	TEMP. NIGHT	LIGHT	PLANTS
1.				
2.				
3.				
4.				
5.				

Figure 5–1

B. Take daytime temperature readings. Place the thermometer in each location for 10 minutes. Record the temperatures in your chart. If possible, take nighttime temperature readings also.

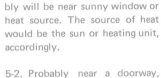 5-1. Which location has the highest temperature? What is the major source of the heat?

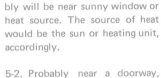 5-2. Which location has the lowest temperature? Why does it have the lowest temperature?

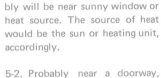 5-3. Which location probably has the greatest temperature change from day to night? Explain why.

The temperature of the air, especially at night, affects plants. And cool or warm drafts affect plants. Some plants grow best in cool places. Some plants grow best in warm places.

The temperature readings that you took probably varied. It is very likely that in one room there are cool, warm, drafty, and non-drafty places. So you should choose plants that will grow best in each place.

C. In Figure 5–2 there are examples of dim, indirect, and direct light. Use these examples to estimate how much light there is in each of the five locations. Then, in your chart for Step A, write *dim, indirect,* or *direct* for each location.

Figure 5–2

5-1. Answers will vary but probably will be near sunny window or heat source. The source of heat would be the sun or heating unit, accordingly.

5-2. Probably near a doorway, open window, or dark part of room because of drafts or lack of light.

5-3. Near the window. The indoor temperature near the window will change as the outside temperature changes.

22   CORE

The amount of light a plant gets is very important. It's the most important factor affecting a plant's health and growth. Too little light will cause a plant's stems to bend and stretch toward a light source. The plant will eventually die, even if it has enough water and fertilizer. Too much light will cause the plant to wilt. Yellow and brown blotches will appear on the leaves.

The plants in your plant wheel have different light requirements. If you don't have a plant wheel, make a list of the first twelve plants in the *Plant Directory.* These are the same plants that are in the plant wheel.

D. In the *Plant Directory,* find the light requirements for the first twelve plants. Then use the symbols from Figure 5–3 to show the light requirements. If you have a plant wheel, the symbol is outlined in each space labeled *light.* Shade the symbols according to Figure 5–3. If you're using a plant list, draw a symbol next to each plant's name.

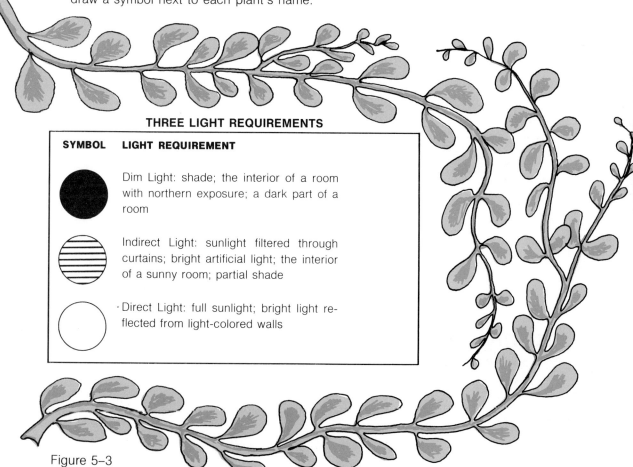

THREE LIGHT REQUIREMENTS

SYMBOL	LIGHT REQUIREMENT
●	Dim Light: shade; the interior of a room with northern exposure; a dark part of a room
◐	Indirect Light: sunlight filtered through curtains; bright artificial light; the interior of a sunny room; partial shade
○	Direct Light: full sunlight; bright light reflected from light-colored walls

Figure 5–3

E. Look at your plant wheel (or list) and your chart from Step A. Match the temperature and light requirements of the plants with the temperature and light of each location. Refer to the *Plant Directory* for the temperature requirements of the plants. Then, in the chart, list the plants that will grow best in each location.

★ **5-4. Which plants need filtered sunlight or bright indirect light?** 5-4. African violet, Areca palm, Boston fern, cacti, coleus, dieffenbachia, ivy, philodendron, rubber tree.

★ **5-5. Which plants need bright sunlight?**

5-5. Cacti, coleus, geranium, ivy.

✔ 5-6. Why are snake plants (sansevieria) and patient Lucy (impatiens) good indoor plants?　5-6. Both plants will grow in places that have bright indirect light to dim light.

★ **5-7. What are the light requirements of cacti, coleus, and ivy?**　5-7. Either direct light or strong indirect light.

Activity 6

MATERIALS PER STUDENT UNIT

Plant Directory

plant wheel from Activity 3, or plant list

*3 plants for plant-watering experiment: 1 water-logged, 1 barely moist, and 1 dry.

*Optional. For directions on preparing plants, see Advance Preparation, pages TM 7 and 8.

For information about the plant-watering experiment, see Advance Preparation, pages TM 7 and 8.

Watering Properly

Plants must have water to live. Some plants need a lot of water; other plants need very little water.

A big problem that plant owners have is how to properly water plants. Overwatering is more common, and causes more plant deaths, than underwatering. A constantly wet soil prevents air from getting to the plant's root system. The roots can't "breathe" properly; the root hairs die; and the plant can't get water and nutrients. Then the leaves wilt and the plant eventually dies.

✔ 6-1. Why does a plant die when its roots have rotted?

6-1. Because the plant can't get air, water, and nutrients from the soil.

If there's a plant-watering experiment set up for you, answer Questions 6-2, 6-3, 6-4. If not, skip the questions and go on.

✔ 6-2. Describe the plant-watering experiment. In your description include the type of plant used, the watering schedule, and the amount of time the experiment has been going on.

6-2. Answers will depend on the experiment used.

✔ 6-3. Compare the overwatered plant to the control plant. Compare the underwatered plant to the control plant.

6-3. Answers will depend on the experiment used.

✔ 6–4. State a conclusion about the effects of different watering schedules on this type of plant.

6-4. Answers will depend on the experiment used.

If you aren't sure about a plant's watering needs, try to find out. Look in the *Plant Directory* or another resource. If you can't find the information, follow this general rule:

> When you water a plant, water it thoroughly. Then let the soil get slightly dry before watering again.

Figure 6–1 shows three ways to water house plants. You might use different ways for different plants, or all three ways for one plant. Figure 6–2 on the next page shows some watering tips. These tips apply to all three methods of watering.

WAYS TO WATER HOUSE PLANTS

1 FROM THE TOP
Water until drops trickle out the drainage hole. Use a can with a long spout so that the leaves won't get wet. Water when there's plenty of light. The light will dry out the plant's crown. Then the crown won't rot. Watering from the top flushes away fertilizer salts that may be on the surface.

2 FROM THE BOTTOM
Water from the bottom only if there is a drainage hole in the pot. Bottom watering lets the soil take as much water as it can hold. Avoid root rot by emptying the saucer 20 to 30 minutes after watering. The pot should never sit in water.

3 SUBMERGE
This method should be used on a very dry plant. Place the entire pot in a bucket of water. The top of the soil should be covered by 2 to 5 cm of water. Remove the pot when the bubbles stop rising. Drain well.

Figure 6–1

WATERING TIPS

1. Use warm water that is at room temperature. Cold water can harm plants.

2. Keep water off the plant's leaves.

3. Plants in plastic pots don't require watering as often as those in clay pots. (Water evaporates through the clay pots.)

4. Water plants in the morning. Then they will have the whole day to use the water.

5. The light, temperature, and humidity of the room affect the moisure in the soil.

Figure 6–2

6-5. Answers will vary. Watering *from the top* or *from the bottom* is practical. Since the soil should be kept wet but not soggy, watering from the bottom might be better.

If students do not have a plant wheel, and you want them to make one, ask them to do the investigation in Activity 3.

★ **6–5. Which watering method would you use for an Areca palm? Why?**

You'll need the following resources to help you learn about the watering needs of common house plants:

Plant Directory
plant wheel from Activity 3 or a list consisting of the first 12 plants in the *Plant Directory*

Use the *Plant Directory* to find the water requirements of the plants. Then draw the symbol for each requirement. Use the symbols shown in Figure 6–3. If you have a plant wheel, the symbol is outlined in each space labeled *water*. Shade the symbols according to Figure 6–3. If you're using a plant list, draw a symbol next to each plant's name.

26 CORE

WATERING HOUSE PLANTS	
SYMBOL	**WATERING REQUIREMENT**
(droplet)	Keep the soil *wet* but not soggy.
(droplet)	Keep the soil *barely moist to moist*.
(droplet)	Let the soil get *fairly dry* between waterings.
(droplet)	Let the soil get *dry*. Water just enough to keep leaves from wilting (about every 4 to 6 weeks).

Figure 6–3

✔ 6–6. Most plants in the *Plant Directory* need barely moist to moist soil. List the plants that have other water requirements.

6-6. Areca palm, cacti, dieffenbachia, sansevieria.

For Questions 6–7 through 6–9, describe the watering needs of each plant shown.

6-7. Boston fern — keep soil barely moist.

6-8. African violet — keep soil barely moist.

★ **6–7.**

★ **6–8.**

★ **6–9.**

6-9. Dieffenbachia — keep soil fairly dry.

Activity 7

MATERIALS PER STUDENT
UNIT
Plant Directory

Plant Problems

You've probably heard this phrase before: *An ounce of prevention is worth a pound of cure.* This is good advice for plant care. By properly taking care of indoor plants, you'll prevent most plant problems. Here are some suggestions to follow:

Provide the right amount of light, water, temperature, and humidity.
Use the right kind of fertilizer.
Regularly inspect and clean the plants.
Use sterile potting soil.

It is difficult to diagnose a plant problem. Any symptom may mean a number of things. Some common problems are caused by poor care. Other problems are caused by pests and disease. In this activity you'll learn the symptoms and treatments of these problems. Get the following resource to help you:

Plant Directory

In your notebook, draw a chart like the one in Figure 7–1. Notice how the chart is organized. Some of the information is given; some is not. Complete the chart for Poor-Care Problems. You'll need to use the Sick Plants Section of the *Plant Directory*.

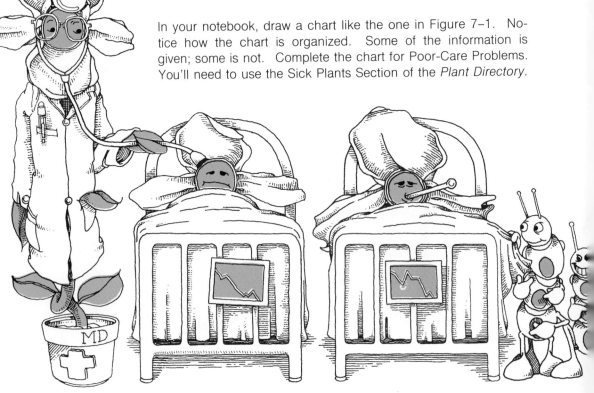

SICK PLANTS				
	MAIN SYMPTOMS	**OTHER SYMPTOMS**	**PROBLEM**	**TREATMENT**
POOR-CARE PROBLEMS	Lower leaves are yellow.		too much water	
	Lower leaves are yellow.		not enough fertilizer	
	Brown or yellow blotches appear on leaves.			
	Brown or yellow blotches appear on leaves.			
	New growth is weak.			
			not enough light	
DISEASE AND PEST PROBLEMS				

Figure 7–1

CORE 29

See Advance Preparation, page TM 8, for suggestions on providing additional experiences for diagnosing plant problems.

Diagnose and suggest treatment for the plant problems shown in Questions 7–1 and 7–2. Use your chart to help you.

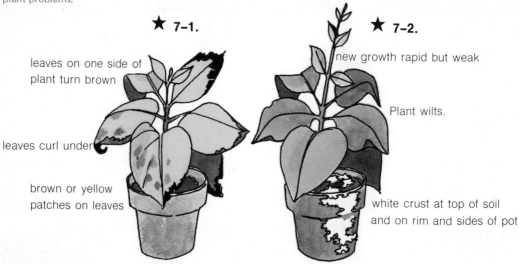

★ 7–1.

leaves on one side of plant turn brown

leaves curl under

brown or yellow patches on leaves

★ 7–2.

new growth rapid but weak

Plant wilts.

white crust at top of soil and on rim and sides of pot

7-1. Too much light — change plant's location so that it gets less light.

7-2. Too much fertilizer — use less fertilizer or fertilize less often.

7-3. Immediately isolate the plant.

7-4. Mealy bugs look like fuzzy bits of cotton; aphids are tiny and crawl. They both can be treated by swabbing with alcohol, washing plant with soap and water, or spraying with malathion.

You may wish to have available one or more empty insecticide containers for students to examine. An empty container of malathion would be useful.

Poor care isn't the only cause of plant problems. Some pests can be troublesome. Often these pests are on newly purchased plants. Sometimes they're on plants that have been outside for awhile. So, when you bring a plant into your home, isolate it for a few weeks. Be sure there are no pests on the plant.

✔ 7–3. Suppose you find pests on a house plant. What is the first thing you should do?

Now complete your chart for Disease and Pest Problems. You'll need to use the Sick Plants section of the *Plant Directory.*

★ **7–4. What symptom distinguishes a mealy bug problem from an aphid problem? How would you treat each problem?**

For all pest problems, the final suggestion is the same: Use an insecticide. The following insecticides are suggested:

rotenone   These natural poisons, made from plants, are
pyrethrum harmless to humans. But rotenone is especially dangerous to fish.

malathion This is very poisonous but decomposes (breaks down) in nature.

30 CORE

HOW TO USE INSECTICIDES

① Read the label carefully. Pay attention to all warnings.

② If the insecticide has to be mixed, mix it carefully according to the directions.

③ If you spill any, wash the area with soap and water.

④ Apply according to the directions for the particular pest and plant. Use in a well-ventilated place. Don't use more than the necessary amount.

⑤ **POISON** Use soap and water to wash the surface on which you sprayed. Wash the container and put it away.

★ **7-5. Suppose you had to use an insecticide on a plant. Describe how you would use it safely.** 7-5. Answers depend on insecticide, but should reflect basic concepts of caution: read directions carefully, wash any spills with soap and water, use in well-ventilated place, use soap and water to wash the container and the surface on which you sprayed.

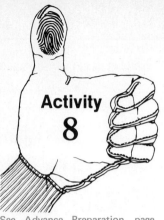

Photosynthesis and Respiration

Activity 8

You may want all students who do this activity to start it on the same day.

If today is Monday or Tuesday, do the preparation for this activity. It's in the following paragraph. Otherwise, go to another activity. Come back to this one on a Monday or Tuesday.

To prepare for this activity, get a healthy coleus plant. Write your name and the date on the pot. Water the plant well. Then place it in complete darkness for at least *three days*. (That's why this preparation must be done on a Monday or Tuesday.) Work on another activity for three days. Then get the plant and begin this activity.

See Advance Preparation, page TM 8, for a suggestion on determining the amount of time to keep your coleus plant in darkness.

MATERIALS PER STUDENT UNIT

1 healthy coleus plant that has been in direct light.
1 healthy coleus plant that has been in darkness for 72 hours
iodine solution, 40 ml
2 heat-resistant beakers (400-600 ml)
colored pencil or crayon
heat-resistant surface
alcohol, 200 ml

3 petri dishes
electric hot plate
tweezers

2 small jars
water
beaker tongs
sharp knife

All living things, including plants, must have food in order to live. We get some or all of our food in a supermarket. Plants get essential elements called *nutrients* [NEW-tree-ents] from the soil. But they make their food themselves. One of the foods plants make is a sugar called *glucose* [GLUE-kos].

Glucose is made by a complicated process called *photosynthesis* [foht-oh-SIN-tha-sis]. For this process, plants need light and *chlorophyll* [KLOR-ah-fill]. Chlorophyll is a chemical substance found in certain green plant cells. During photosynthesis, water and carbon dioxide are combined and form glucose. As the glucose molecules are made, oxygen is given off. See Figure 8–1.

32 CORE

PHOTOSYNTHESIS

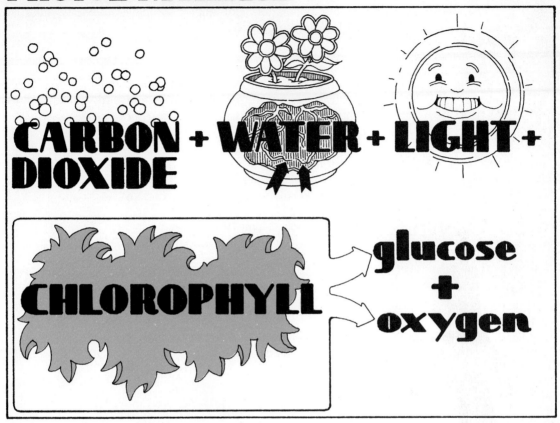

Figure 8–1

★ **8–1. What chemical substance is found in certain plant cells and is needed for photosynthesis to occur?**

8-1. Chlorophyll.

Wherever there is chlorophyll in a plant, photosynthesis is going on. Photosynthesis takes place mainly in the leaves. But green stems make food too. Nearly all the food molecules produced are glucose molecules. If the plant needs food, it uses the glucose molecules right away. Otherwise, the molecules are clumped together to form starch. The starch is stored and when the plant needs food, the starch is changed back to glucose.

✔ 8–2. Suppose you found starch in a plant leaf. What process probably took place there? 8-2. Photosynthesis.

✔ 8–3. Suppose you found starch in one part of a leaf and not in another. Explain what this could mean.

8-3. Photosynthesis occurred in the part where starch was found but not in the other part.

glucose molecules

starch molecule

CORE 33

The coleus is an interesting plant. Not all parts of its leaves contain chlorophyll. Because of this feature, you'll use coleus to study the effects of light and chlorophyll in photosynthesis. You'll need these materials:

electric hot plate
2 heat-resistant beakers, 400–600 ml each
healthy coleus plant that's been in direct light
healthy coleus plant that's been in darkness for at least 3 days
sharp knife
colored pencil or crayon
tweezers
beaker tongs
heat-resistant surface
alcohol, 200 ml
3 petri dishes
iodine solution, 40 ml
2 small jars, each filled with cool water

A. Set up a hot plate in a *well-ventilated* area. Fill the beaker 1/3 full of water. Place the beaker on the hot plate. Set the hot plate for medium heat and wait for the water to boil.

See Advance Preparation, page TM 8, for directions on preparing an iodine solution.

If a hot plate is not available, make a double boiler. Proceed as follows: Fill a heat-resistant beaker about ¾ full of alcohol. Put the beaker in a heat-resistant container. Pour water in the container so that the water level is the same as the alcohol level in the beaker. Use a burner and heat until the alcohol boils.

B. While waiting for the water to boil, get the coleus plants. Cut one medium-size well-colored leaf from each plant. Notch the leaf that has been in the light.

C. Sketch each leaf. Outline and shade the nongreen portions of the leaves in your sketches. Label the notched-leaf sketch *in the light*. Label the other sketch *in the dark*. Then label both sketches *BEFORE*. Repeat this procedure. This time don't shade portions of the leaves. Label these drawings *AFTER.*

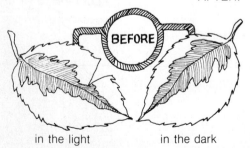

in the light   in the dark

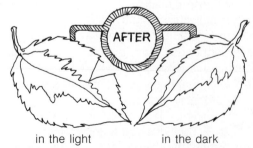

in the light   in the dark

D. When the water boils turn the heat to low. Use the tweezers to submerge both leaves. Keep them submerged for about 1 minute. This will kill the leaves and soften them.

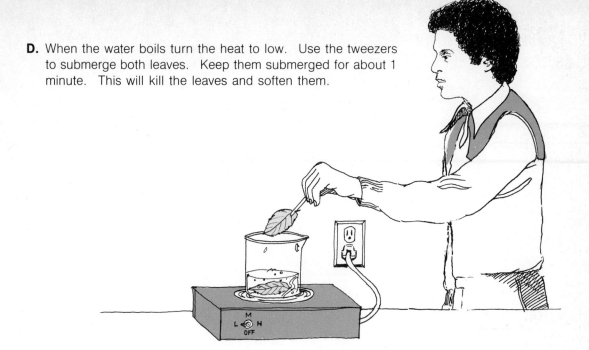

E. Use beaker tongs to remove the beaker from the hot plate. Put the beaker on a heat-resistant surface. Fill the other beaker 1/3 full of alcohol and place it on the hot plate.

CAUTION

Be very careful when removing the boiling water from the hot plate. And be very careful when placing the beaker of alcohol on the hot plate.

DO NOT BREATHE THE FUMES FROM THE ALCOHOL. And keep all flames away from the fumes.

F. When the alcohol boils, turn off the hot plate. Use the tweezers to transfer the leaves from the water to the boiling alcohol.

G. Keep the leaves in the alcohol until they turn pale, about 2 to 3 minutes. Then use tweezers to transfer the leaves back to the beaker of water. Keep the leaves in the water for about 1 minute.

H. Use the tweezers to place each leaf in a separate petri dish. Cover the leaves with about 15 ml of iodine solution.

Let the leaves soak for 3 to 4 minutes. Then, using the tweezers, rinse each leaf in a jar of cool water. Place both leaves on the clean petri dish.

IMPORTANT: Iodine will stain your skin and clothing. Use it very carefully.

Observe the results of your treatment. The iodine causes any starch in the leaf to turn dark blue or black. In the *AFTER* sketches that you drew, shade the leaves to show where starch is located.

The leaf that was kept in the light, the notched leaf, is the *control* leaf.

✔ 8-4. In the control leaf, where is chlorophyll present? How do you know?

✔ 8-5. In the control leaf, where is chlorophyll absent?

The leaf that was kept in the dark is the *experimental* leaf.

✔ 8-6. How does the experimental leaf show that light is necessary for photosynthesis?

The coleus plant that was in the dark had been in the light at one time. So it must have had starch stored in its leaves *before* it was put in the dark. Where did the starch go?

✔ 8-7. How do plants use stored starch?

8-4. Chlorophyll is present in the areas that were green or dark red. When iodine was applied, these areas turned dark blue or black indicating the presence of starch, and therefore, chlorophyll.

8-5. In the areas of the leaf that were white or very light in color.

8-6. The green and dark red areas of the experimental leaf did not turn dark blue when iodine was applied. So starch was not present and photosynthesis did not occur in those areas. Since light was the only missing factor in the experimental plant, light must be necessary for photosynthesis.

8-7. They change the starch to glucose and use the glucose.

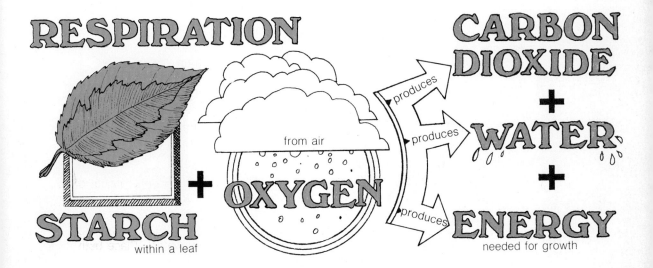

RESPIRATION

STARCH
within a leaf

+ OXYGEN
from air

produces
produces
produces

CARBON DIOXIDE
+
WATER
+
ENERGY
needed for growth

Plants get energy when they use the food they make. They need the energy to live and grow. The process of getting energy from food is called *respiration.* It's a complicated process. The starch in the leaf or stem is changed to glucose and combined with oxygen from the air. Carbon dioxide and water are released to the air. Useful energy is provided to the plant for growth.

Photosynthesis and respiration are going on: Plants are manufacturing, storing, and using food.

Respiration is going on: Plants are using food.

8-8. A plant must have light in order for photosynthesis to go on. Without light, the process stops.

★ **8–8. Why can't photosynthesis go on in the dark?**

✔ 8–9. In your investigation you studied a coleus plant that had been in the dark. What happened to the starch stored in the leaves of that plant?

8-9. The starch was used up during respiration.

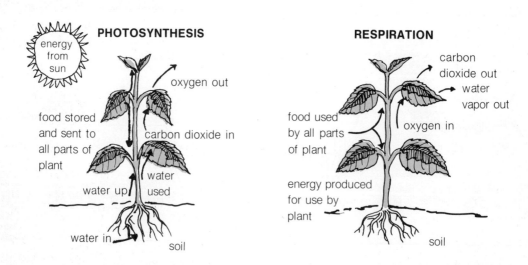

PHOTOSYNTHESIS

energy from sun

oxygen out

food stored and sent to all parts of plant

carbon dioxide in

water up | water used

water in | soil

RESPIRATION

carbon dioxide out | water vapor out

food used by all parts of plant

oxygen in

energy produced for use by plant

soil

8-10. During photosynthesis, food is produced; during respiration, plants get energy from the food.

★ **8–10. Explain the differences between photosynthesis and respiration.**

38 CORE

PHOTOSYNTHESIS
35%–60% of the world's photosynthesis is carried on by microscopic plants that live in water. The rest of the world's photosynthesis is produced by all the other types of land and water plants. It is estimated that the world's plants produce about 10–100 billion tons of oxygen every year. Animals need oxygen to live.

We get most of our food from plants that grow on land. We preserve these food products to feed ourselves.

We can't digest part of some plants, such as grass. But many animals can. We eat the meat of some of these animals. We also get products like milk and cheese from some of these animals.

The parts of the plant that we can't digest are *cellulose* and *silica compounds*.

★ **8–11. Suppose someone said, "Humans can't survive without photosynthesis." Would you agree or disagree? Why?**

8-11. Agree. Photosynthesis produces the oxygen we breathe and the food we eat. Without food or oxygen, we couldn't survive.

ACTIVITY EMPHASIS: Presented in this activity are experiments with grass shoots. These experiments help explain phototropism and also give students practice in identifying conclusions that are supported by observations.

Plant Growth Experiments

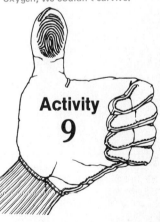

Activity 9

MATERIALS PER STUDENT UNIT
None.

Plants (except for bacteria) must have light to live. Without light, they cannot make food and they die. It seems that plants can "sense" where light is. They tend to grow toward light.

Growing toward light is called *phototropism* [foe-ta-TRO-piz-cm]. *Photo* refers to light; *tropism* to turning. One of the first people to investigate phototropism was Charles Darwin in the late 1800's. You've probably heard of Charles Darwin before. He is well-known for ideas about how life changed through time.

Darwin observed that the tiny shoots sprouting from grass seeds would bend toward light. He did experiments to try to explain how this bending happened. During the next fifty years, scientists in many countries continued the work Darwin started. Finally, an explanation of the bending process was worked out.

tray of seedlings covered by box

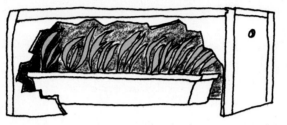 

The purpose of these experiments is not for students to understand the cause of plants bending towards the light, but rather for students to justify scientific conclusions.

In this activity you'll follow several early experiments that were done to explain phototropism. The experiments are illustrated, the observations listed, and the conclusions discussed.

EXPERIMENT 1 CUTTING OFF THE TIPS

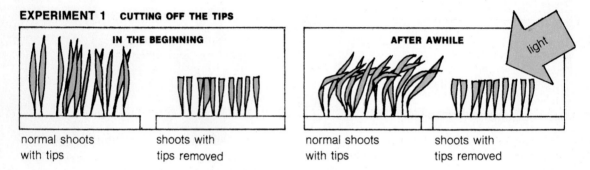

IN THE BEGINNING

AFTER AWHILE

light

normal shoots with tips

shoots with tips removed

normal shoots with tips

shoots with tips removed

OBSERVATIONS: The normal shoots bend toward the light. The shoots with tips removed do not bend toward the light.

EXPERIMENT 2 COVERING THE TIPS

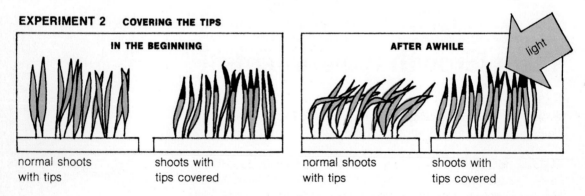

IN THE BEGINNING

AFTER AWHILE

light

normal shoots with tips

shoots with tips covered

normal shoots with tips

shoots with tips covered

OBSERVATIONS: The normal shoots bend toward the light. The shoots with the covered tips do not bend toward the light.

Now let's consider and analyze possible conclusions for both Experiments 1 and 2.

CONCLUSION 1: Cutting off the tips injured the shoots so that they couldn't bend.

ANALYSIS: This conclusion *is not supported* by the observations. The shoots with covered tips were not injured and they did not bend toward the light.

CONCLUSION 2: The tip is sensitive to light. The tip somehow causes the bending.

ANALYSIS: This conclusion *is supported* by the observations. When light couldn't get to the tip, the shoots did not bend.

EXPERIMENT 3 USING AN AGAR BLOCK

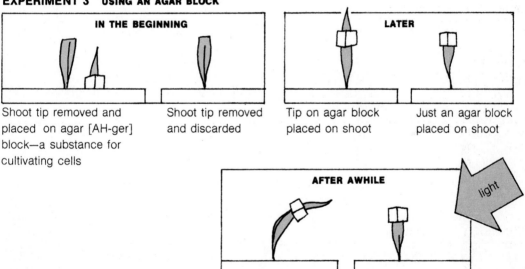

IN THE BEGINNING

Shoot tip removed and placed on agar [AH-ger] block—a substance for cultivating cells

Shoot tip removed and discarded

LATER

Tip on agar block placed on shoot

Just an agar block placed on shoot

AFTER AWHILE

light

OBSERVATIONS: The shoot with the tip and agar block bends toward the light. The shoot with just the agar block does not bend.

CONCLUSION: The agar block caused the shoot to bend.

✔ 9-1. Look at the conclusion for Experiment 3. Is it supported by the observations for Experiment 3? Explain your answer.

9-1. No. If the conclusion was supported by the observation, both shoots would have bent toward the light (both shoots had agar blocks on them).

EXPERIMENT 4   USING AN AGAR BLOCK

IN THE BEGINNING	LATER	AFTER AWHILE
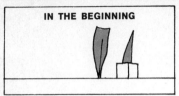	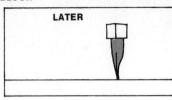	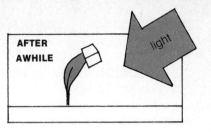

The shoot tip is cut off and placed on a block of agar. The tip is left on the agar block for awhile.

The tip is removed from the agar block. The block is placed on the shoot.

OBSERVATION: The shoot bends toward the light.

CONCLUSION: A substance from the shoot's tip moved into the agar. Then the substance moved into the shoot and caused the shoot to bend.

9-2. Yes. The shoot and agar bent toward the light as long as the shoot's tip had been in contact with the agar. Agar alone did not cause bending.

✔ 9-2. Is the conclusion for Experiment 4 supported by the observations from Experiments 3 and 4? Explain your answer.

Now consider this conclusion:

CONCLUSION: Experiments 1 through 4 show that all plants produce a substance which causes the bending response to light (phototropism).

ANALYSIS: Whoa! This conclusion *is not supported*. The conclusion seems true only for grass shoots, not for *all* plants.

EXPERIMENT 5

IN THE BEGINNING	LATER
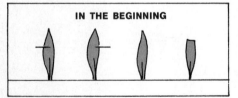	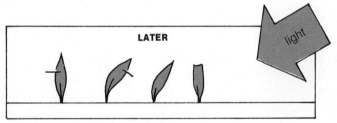

A sliver of glass is inserted into different sides of 2 shoots—tip is removed from 1 shoot.

9-3. All three conclusions, *a, b,* and *c,* are not supported.

★ **9-3. Which of the following conclusions are not supported by the results of Experiment 5?**
a. The thin piece of glass caused the shoot to bend toward the light.
b. The thin piece of glass had no effect on the bending of the shoots.
c. Something produced in the tip caused the bending toward the light.

✔ 9-4. Consider the results of Experiments 1 through 4. Use these results and your observations for Experiment 5 to explain what happened in Experiment 5.

Scientists have identified the substances that cause phototropism. What these substances are and how they cause bending is discussed in *Activity 14, Plant Hormones.*

9-4. In the tips of grass shoots there's a substance that's sensitive to light and causes the shoots to bend toward the light. From Experiment 5 it appears that the substance collects in the side *away* from the light causing the shoot to bend. The glass sliver on that side prevented the substance from collecting. Thus, the shoot didn't bend.

Activity
10

What's Normal?

ACTIVITY EMPHASIS: Presented in this activity are simulated data on growth measurements. The data are used to explain normal distribution of plant features.

Jack, Anita, and Tony are working on a science project. They are investigating how plants grow. Six weeks ago the students planted some coleus seeds in a large tray. They kept the soil moist. The seeds sprouted in about ten days. Then the students made growth measurements on the seedlings. The data are listed in the chart on page 44.

MATERIALS PER STUDENT
UNIT
Resource Unit 4
Resource Unit 19

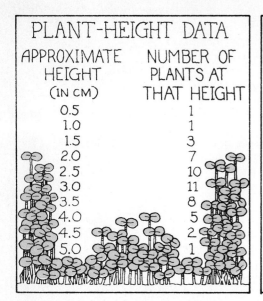

PLANT-HEIGHT DATA

APPROXIMATE HEIGHT (IN CM)	NUMBER OF PLANTS AT THAT HEIGHT
0.5	1
1.0	1
1.5	3
2.0	7
2.5	10
3.0	11
3.5	8
4.0	5
4.5	2
5.0	1

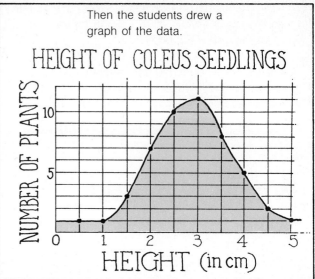

Then the students drew a graph of the data.

HEIGHT OF COLEUS SEEDLINGS

Notice the curve is somewhat bell-shaped. That is, the highest part of the curve is the middle part; the lowest parts are at each end. The shape of a curve depends on the distribution of the data. Jack, Anita, and Tony have data that are in a normal (bell-shaped) distribution. The graph of the data is called a *normal distribution curve* or a *normal curve*.

Most of the plants seem to be the same height, about 3 centimetres. But there are a few plants taller than that and a few shorter.

I wonder if there are other plant features that vary like height does: if other measurements have a normal distribution.

Let's find out if the lengths of the leaves are in a normal distribution.

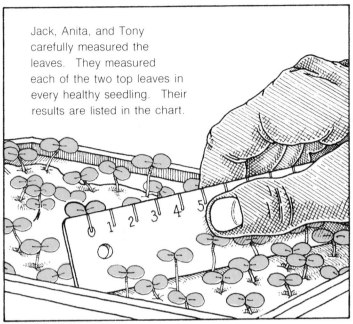

Jack, Anita, and Tony carefully measured the leaves. They measured each of the two top leaves in every healthy seedling. Their results are listed in the chart.

LEAF-LENGTH DATA	
APPROXIMATE LENGTH OF LEAF (in cm)	NUMBER OF LEAVES AT THAT LENGTH
0.1	1
0.2	3
0.3	6
0.4	11
0.5	16
0.6	20
0.7	18
0.8	11
0.9	6
1.0	3
1.1	1
1.2	1
1.3	1

✔ 10-1. Make a graph of the leaf-length data. Label the vertical axis *Number of Leaves* and the horizontal axis *Length of Leaves*. If you have trouble drawing the graph, do *Resource Unit 4*.

✔ 10-2. Are the leaf-length data in a normal distribution? How can you tell?

★ **10-3. Suppose the students investigated the following features of the coleus seedlings. Which features do you think would be in a normal distribution?**
a. seedling weight
b. root length
c. number of roots

As plants grow, some develop faster or slower than others. The weight, root length, number of leaves, height, and leaf size vary from plant to plant. All measurements related to growth are in a normal distribution.

This may be the first time you've met normal distribution. If so, don't worry if the meaning isn't completely clear. You'll study normal distribution again in other minicourses. However, if you've seen it before and are feeling uneasy, you may want to do *Resource Unit 19*. It describes normal distribution in more detail.

10-1. The curve should be bell-shaped. The highest point should be at *Length 0.6* and *Number 20;* the lowest points at *Length 0.1* and *Number 1; Length 1.1* and *Number 1; Length 1.2* and *Number 1; Length 1.3* and *Number 1.*

10-2. Yes. The graph of the data is a normal curve.

10-3. a, b, c

Activity 11

ACTIVITY EMPHASIS: Students use their knowledge about identification and care of house plants to plan the "greening" of a room. They match the light, temperature, and humidity conditions of the room with the requirements of the plants.

MATERIALS PER STUDENT UNIT
None.

Greening a Room

This activity could serve as a capstone activity for the minicourse. You may wish to have students do all the activities that they plan to do (core, advanced, or excursion) before beginning this one.

Now you know how to identify, propagate, and take care of indoor plants. Here you'll use the knowledge to "green a room."

Choose a room you'd like to decorate. Consider these questions:

How do you want the room to look?
What are the best growing conditions for the plants?

Draw a floor plan of the room you chose. (See Figure 11–1.) Your plan should have the following information:
a. the approximate dimensions of the room; the dimensions and locations of any windows and doors
b. the location of any heating units such as radiators or baseboard units; the location of large pieces of furniture
c. the direction that each window faces (north, northeast . . .)
d. places where the temperature is high or low; and if it's obvious, places where humidity is high or low
e. the type of lighting; the color of the walls, floor (or rugs), furniture, and curtains

Use ◯ for direct light,
⊖ for indirect light,
● for dim light.

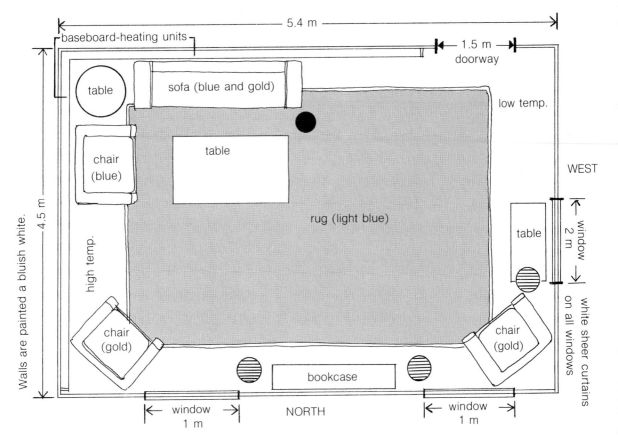

Figure 11–1

Now choose six or more kinds of plants to put in the room. Choose plants that have different shapes and colors; variety will add beauty and interest to the room. Choose plants that can grow well in the room. Match the temperature, light, and humidity requirements of the plants with the conditions of the room.

Find suitable places for the plants that you choose. Locate each plant in your floor plan. You may want to sketch the plants right on the floor plan. If so, label each plant. Or you may want to prepare a "key" using a symbol for each plant. Then you'd draw the symbol right on the floor plan.

Describe the plants that you selected. For each plant include:
a. the common or scientific name of the plant.
b. the approximate size (length and width) and color of the leaves; the approximate size (diameter) of the flower.
c. light, water, humidity, and temperature requirements.

Give your floor plan and plant descriptions to your teacher to check.

advanced

Activity 12 Planning

If you need to do Activity 14, do it first. Then do the other activities in any order.

Activity 13 Page 50

Objective 14: Describe the light and dark reactions of photosynthesis.

Sample Question: Which statements are true about the light reactions of photosynthesis? The light reactions
a. *take place in the chloroplasts.*
b. *produce glucose from CO_2 and H_2O.*
c. *produce oxygen from H_2O.*
d. *use chlorophyll to absorb light energy.*

Objective 15: Identify the roles of chlorophyll, CO_2, H_2O, ATP, and NADP in photosynthesis.

Sample Question: Match each plant substance with its role in photosynthesis.

SUBSTANCE	ROLE
a. *CO_2*	1. *Loses oxygen.*
b. *H_2O*	2. *Carries hydrogen.*
c. *NADP*	3. *Combines with hydrogen to make glucose.*
d. *ATP*	4. *Absorbs light energy.*
e. *Chlorophyll*	5. *Stores energy.*

Activity 14 Page 55

Objective 16: Explain how auxins cause phototropism and geotropism.

Sample Question: How does the hormone auxin cause a plant to bend toward light?

a. by causing more plant cells to grow on the side away from the light
b. by causing plant cells to become longer on the side away from the light
c. by causing plant cells to shorten on the side nearest the light

Objective 17: Describe how auxins can affect plant growth.

Sample Question: How do auxins that are produced in the growing tips and leaves of a plant affect a plant?

a. by causing roots to grow
b. by causing the stem to bend toward gravity
c. by limiting branching and bushiness

Activity 15 page 59

Objective 18: Identify the meaning of adhesion, cohesion, root pressure, and transpiration.

Sample Question: Match each process with its description.

PROCESS	DESCRIPTION
a. Adhesion	1. Results from diffusion into roots
b. Cohesion	2. Loss of water vapor from leaves
c. Root pressure	3. Attraction of unlike molecules for each other
d. Transpiration	4. Attraction of like molecules for each other

Objective 19: Explain how water is moved from a plant's roots to its leaves.

Sample Question: Which process provides the "pull" for moving the water in the xylem of plants?

a. adhesion
b. cohesion
c. root pressure
d. transpiration

Answers
14. a,c,d 15. a-3, b-1, c-2, d-5, e-4
16. b 17. a,c 18. a-3, b-4, c-1, d-2
19. d

Inside the Photosynthesis Factory

Activity
13

MATERIALS PER STUDENT
UNIT
microscope
prepared slide of leaf cross section
Resource Unit 3

Students may want to prepare slides of leaf cross sections. For directions, see Advance Preparation, pages TM 8 and 9.

The main "chemical factories" of a plant are the leaves. It is mostly in the leaves that the *photosynthesis* process takes place. During this process the light energy of the sun is used to produce food molecules.

In this activity you're going to learn what happens inside a leaf cell during photosynthesis. First you'll need to understand the structure of a leaf. Get the following materials:

   microscope
   prepared slide of leaf cross section

If you are not sure about how to use a microscope, do *Resource Unit 3* before continuing with this activity.

A. Look at the leaf cross-section under low power and then under high power. In your notebook sketch what you see under high power.

B. Your sketch should be similar to the leaf cross-section in Figure 13–1. Certain parts of the leaf are labeled in Figure 13–1. Find these parts in your sketch and label them.

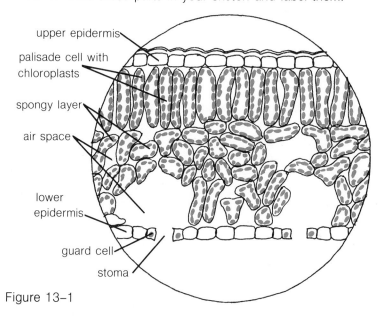

upper epidermis
palisade cell with chloroplasts
spongy layer
air space
lower epidermis
guard cell
stoma

Figure 13–1

Shown in Figure 13–2 is part of a palisade cell under greater magnification than you can get with your microscope. Within a palisade cell there can be seen separate structures called *chloroplasts.* The chloroplasts contain all the chlorophyll of the leaf. In most plants all the reactions of photosynthesis occur in the chloroplasts.

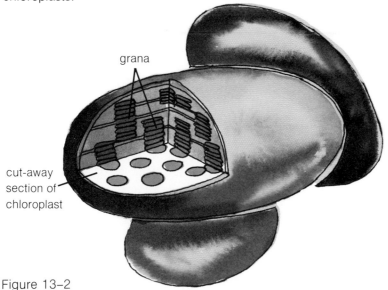

grana

cut-away section of chloroplast

Figure 13–2

Chloroplasts contain structures made of stacked hollow discs. These structures are called *grana.* (One such structure is called a *granum.*) The grana are involved in the reaction with light. An electron microscope provides greater detail of the grana, as shown in Figure 13–3.

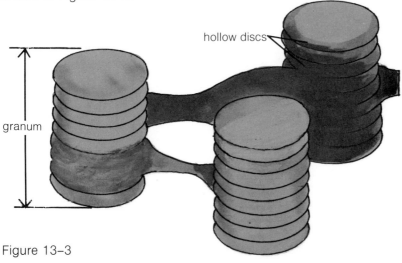

hollow discs

granum

Figure 13–3

✔ 13–1. What substance is found in the grana?

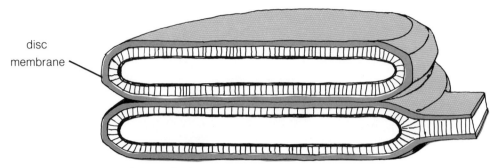

disc
membrane

Figure 13–4

Scientists think the membrane (wall) of each hollow disc is made of granular units. (See Figure 13–4.)   Each of these units may contain about 300 chlorophyll molecules.

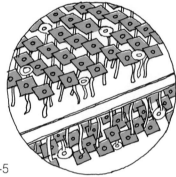

Figure 13–5

Figure 13–5 shows a stylized view of the molecules in one granular unit.   The chlorophyll molecules, along with a few other molecules, absorb the light energy.   Then the chlorophyll passes on the energy for use in the chemical reactions of photosynthesis.

✔ 13–2. Think of the leaf as a group of chemical factories. Where is the photosynthesis factory located?

Photosynthesis is a series of chemical reactions that can be divided into two sets: light reactions and dark reactions.   The light reactions need light energy in order to happen; the dark reactions do not need light energy but they're normally coupled to the light reactions.   Both sets of reactions occur at the same time.   In Figure 13–6, the dark reactions are shaded; the chlorophyll which has absorbed the light energy is labeled *high-energy chlorophyll.*

52 ADVANCED

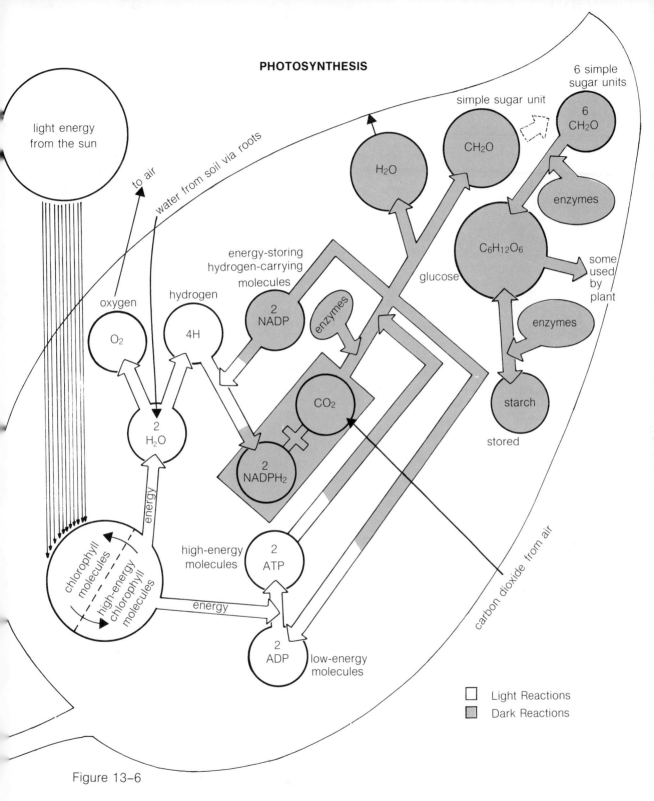

PHOTOSYNTHESIS

Figure 13-6

Follow Figure 13–6 in order to answer these questions:

✔ 13–3. What happens to the chlorophyll when it absorbs light energy? 13-3. It becomes high-energy chlorophyll.

★ **13–4. High-energy chlorophyll can lose its energy. What happens to this energy?** 13-4. It is used to break down water molecules and change the ADP molecules to ATP molecules.

✔ 13–5. What happens to an ADP molecule when it gets energy? 13-5. It is transformed into a high-energy ATP molecule.

✔ 13–6. What happens to the hydrogen atoms that come from the water molecule? 13-6. They join with NADP to make $NADPH_2$.

✔ 13–7. In the dark reactions, where does the carbon dioxide come from? 13-7. From the air.

★ **13–8. What happens to $NADPH_2$ and ATP when the simple sugar unit, CH_2O, is made?** 13-8. |$NADPH_2$ loses its hydrogen and becomes NADP. ATP loses its energy and becomes ADP.'

✔ 13–9. How is the simple sugar unit converted into glucose and starch? 13-9. By means of enzymes.

✔ 13–10. Where does the oxygen come from that is given off during photosynthesis? 13-10. From the water molecules when they are broken down.

✔ 13–11. Where does the oxygen in the glucose and simple sugar come from? 13-11. From CO_2.

★ **13–12. Listed below are results from the light reactions and the dark reactions of photosynthesis. Which results are from the light reactions? Which are from the dark reactions?**

a. Oxygen (O_2) is released.

b. Simple sugar units (CH_2O) are made into glucose and starch.

c. Carbon dioxide (CO_2) is used to form the simple sugar units (CH_2O).

d. Water (H_2O) is broken down to oxygen (O_2) and hydrogen (H).

13-12. Light reactions: a, d; Dark reactions: b, c.

Plant Hormones

Scientists have found chemical substances in plants that affect plant functions. These substances are called *hormones*. The hormones that control growth are called *auxins* [AWK-sins]. The auxin *indoleacetic* [IN-dole-a-seat-ik] *acid* seems to control *phototropism,* the bending or growing toward a source of light.

In the following investigation, you'll learn how auxins work. You'll need about 45 minutes for this investigation. Get these materials:

> 2 potted coleus plants, 20–30 cm tall, with straight stems
> auxin paste
> glass stirring rod
> masking tape

A. Get one of the plants. This will be the experimental plant. Dip the glass rod into the auxin paste. Then rub some paste on one side of the stem, about 1 to 2 cm from the top. Put a small piece of masking tape right below the smear. This is to mark the location of the smear. The other plant is the control plant. Do nothing to it.

B. Place both the experimental and control plants in the dark. Work on another activity for the rest of the class period. At the end of class, take out the plants and look for changes.

✔ 14–1. Describe what happened to the plant that was rubbed with auxin paste. Compare it to the control plant. What differences do you observe?

MATERIALS PER STUDENT UNIT
2 potted coleus plants, 20-30 cm tall, well-rooted and with straight stems
3 young coleus cuttings[1]
auxin paste[2]
glass stirring rod
masking tape, 10 cm
grease pencil

1. Be sure to have cuttings available for those students who did not make 3 cuttings in Activity 2.

2. See Advance Preparation, page TM 9, for the preparation of auxin paste.

14-1. The plant bends away from the side with auxin paste. The control plant does not bend.

PHOTOTROPISM

Light causes auxins on this side of the stem to move to the opposite side.

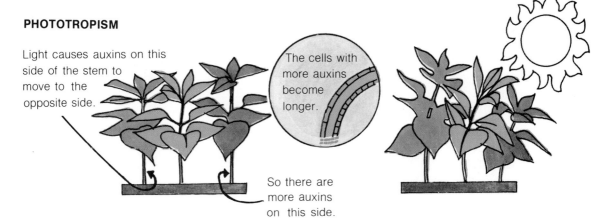

The cells with more auxins become longer.

So there are more auxins on this side.

Auxins are produced in the growing tips of stems and roots, and in young buds, leaves, and flowers. Scientists believe that auxins can affect plant growth in two ways: by causing an increase in the number of plant cells or a change in the length of a cell. The effect auxins have depends on the type of plant cell and the amount of auxins present.

14-2. Light causes auxins to collect on the side of the stem that's farthest from the light. The cells with more auxins grow faster than the other cells. This causes the plant to bend toward the light.

★ 14–2. How do auxins produce phototropism?

Florists and gardeners pinch (squeeze) off the growing tips of plants. Do you know why? Find out by doing the following investigation. You'll need these materials:

3 young coleus cuttings, about the same size, from Activity 2
masking tape for labeling
grease pencil
auxin paste
glass stirring rod

A. Number the plants *1, 2,* and *3.* Do nothing to Plant 1. It is the control plant. Pinch off the growing tip at the top of the stem in Plant 2. Keep pinching off any new growth that appears near the growing tip.

growing
tip

B. Pinch off the growing tip at the top of the stem in Plant 3. Keep pinching off any new growth near the growing tip. Every day use the glass rod to put a dab of auxin paste where the tip was. Wash the rod after using it.

For the next week or two, continue to pinch off any new growth near the growing tips of Plants 2 and 3; continue to dab auxin paste on Plant 3. When there are noticeable differences among Plants 1, 2, and 3, answer Questions 14–3 and 14–4.

✔ 14–3. Describe the appearance of Plants 1, 2, and 3.

★ **14–4. Explain how auxins influence "bushiness" in a plant.**

14-3. Plants 1 and 3 kept growing, mostly at the top. Plant 2 grew by branching out from the sides.

14-4. Auxins, produced in the growing tips, seem to inhibit bushiness. Without the auxins in the growing tip, other parts of the plant grow, making the plant more bushy.

As you learned, plants respond to a light source. Plants also respond to gravity. The bending or turning toward gravity is called *geotropism* [gee-AH-tro-piz-em]. If the plant growth is toward gravity, the growth is *positively geotropic*. If the growth is away from gravity, the growth is *negatively geotropic.*

Suppose you put a young plant on its side in a dark place, as in Figure 14–1. The force of gravity could cause an increase in the amount of auxins in the lower side of the plant's leaves or stems.

The roots and leaves are relatively straight.

In a few days, the roots grow downward; the leaves and stems grow upward.

GRAVITY

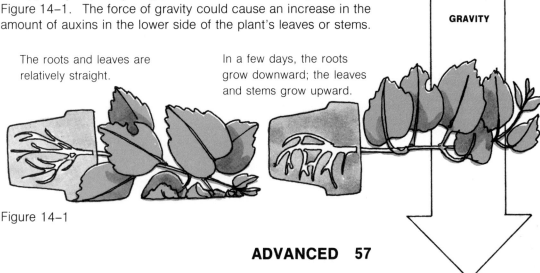

Figure 14–1

14-5. The auxins, collecting on the lower side of the stems and leaves, cause the cells to grow faster. This causes the stems and leaves to bend upward.

★ **14–5. Look at Figure 14–1 (page 57). How could auxins cause the upward growth (negative geotropism) of the stems and leaves?**

Suppose the auxins in a plant's roots respond to gravity in the same way as auxins in the stems and leaves. Then gravity should cause an increase in the amount of auxins in the lower side of the root. Therefore, the root should grow upward. What actually happens is shown in Figure 14–2.

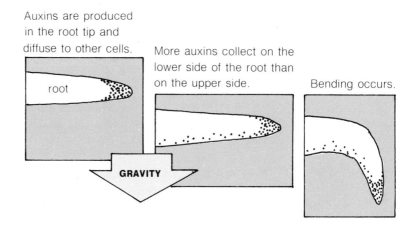

Auxins are produced in the root tip and diffuse to other cells.

root

GRAVITY

More auxins collect on the lower side of the root than on the upper side.

Bending occurs.

Figure 14–2

Notice that the root grows *downward.* Recall that the stem and leaves grew upward (Figure 14–1). Why the roots react the way they do is not yet known. One theory is that too much auxin can *inhibit* cell growth and cell elongation in roots. But is this theory sound? Consider these experiments.

EXPERIMENT 1

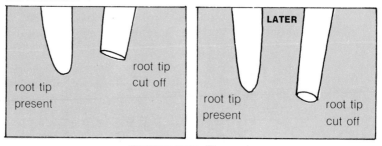

root tip present

root tip cut off

LATER

root tip present

root tip cut off

OBSERVATION: The root without a root tip showed more growth.

58 ADVANCED

EXPERIMENT 2

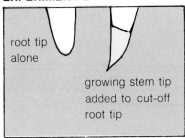

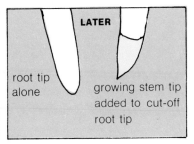

OBSERVATION: The root with the stem tip added showed less growth.

MATERIALS PER STUDENT
UNIT
fresh stalk of celery with leaves or
   a leafy stem from a coleus plant
single-edged razor blade or a knife
magnifying glass or hand lens
soap
glass stirring rod
microscope slide
medicine dropper
glass capillary tube, 10-cm long
jar, small
masking tape, 5 cm
jar, about 1-litre
food coloring
Resource Unit 12

★ **14-6. Describe how auxins may cause the geotropic response of roots.** 14-6. In roots, auxins seem to *retard* growth. as observed in Experiments 1 and 2. Thus, in a horizontal root, auxins would collect on the lower side and retard the growth of the cells. Cells on the upper side would grow faster than those on the lower side and the root would bend downward.

Plant Plumbing

Activity
15

ACTIVITY EMPHASIS: Students investigate the effects of adhesion, cohesion, diffusion, root pressure, and transpiration in plants.

Begin this activity on any day but a Friday. The first investigation must be started one day and finished the next.

Grass, trees, and most other plants get nearly all the water they need through their roots. How does the water get to the topmost leaves? This activity will help you to answer that question. First do the following investigation. You'll need these materials:

large jar, about 1-litre capacity
masking tape for labeling
food coloring
fresh stalk of celery, with leaves, or a leaf-bearing stem from a
   healthy coleus plant
sharp knife
magnifying glass or hand lens

Celery is recommended for this investigation. Be sure the stalk is fresh and that it has leaves. Freshness insures the occurrence of active water transport through the vascular system.

Instead of food coloring, eosin, fuchsine, methylene blue, or methylene red dyes may be used for this investigation.

A. Label the jar and fill it with water. Add several drops of food coloring. Then submerge the stalk and swish it around to stir the water. Cut off part of the stalk as shown in the drawing.

Set the jar where it will be undisturbed and go on to a different activity. Come back to this investigation during your next science class.

Cut 0.5 cm from end.

ADVANCED 59

If color is not apparent, have student cut the stalk again — 0.5 cm to 1 cm higher. Or, have student start over with a fresher stalk.

B. When color shows up in the leaves, cut the stalk and a leaf as shown in the drawing. Use a hand lens or magnifying glass to examine the cut ends of the stalk and the leaf.

15-1. Answers will vary. Sketch and description should show color in "tubes" of the stalk and in veins of the leaves.

15-2. The color is concentrated in small circular areas suggesting tubes.

✔ 15–1. In your notebook, describe the magnified cut ends of the stem and leaf. Then sketch the cut ends. Show where the color appears.

✔ 15–2. What evidence is there that the colored water moved through tubes in the plant?

You've observed water carrying tubes that exist in non-woody, *herbaceous* [er-BAY-shus], stems. Woody-stemmed plants, such as trees and bushes, also have tubes for moving water. Magnified cross-sections of a woody stem and an herbaceous stem are shown in Figure 15–1.

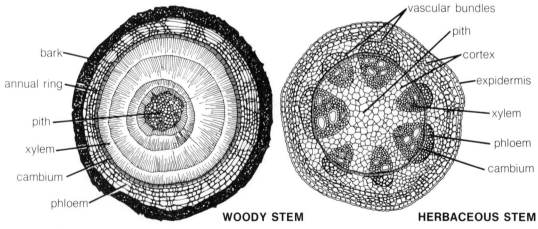

WOODY STEM   HERBACEOUS STEM

Figure 15–1

✔ 15–3. What structures do the woody and herbaceous stems have in common?

15-3. Phloem, pith, cambium, and xylem.

The *phloem* [FLOW-em] carries the food produced in the leaves to all parts of the plant. The *xylem* [ZEYE-lem] carries water and dissolved minerals from the roots to all parts of the plant. The xylem also serves to strengthen the stem. The *cambium* [KAM-be-um] is the growing area of the plant: New cells for the phloem and xylem are produced in the cambium.

✔ 15–4. The arrangement of the cambium, xylem, and phloem differs in woody and herbaceous plants. Describe the differences.

15-4. In woody stems the cambium, xylem, and phloem form a band or "ring" around the stem. In herbaceous stems these structures are grouped in areas called vascular bundles. The bundles are in a circular formation around the center of the stem.

It was the xylem tubes that carried the colored water through the stalk and leaf. But *how* did the liquid move upward through the xylem? In order to answer this question, certain properties of water must be studied. You'll need the following materials:

microscope slide
soap
medicine dropper
glass capillary tube, about 10 cm long
small jar
food coloring
glass stirring rod

The smaller the diameter of the capillary tube, the better the results will be.

A. Scrub the microscope slide with soapy water; rinse and dry it completely. Then use the medicine dropper to put one drop of water on the slide.

✔ 15–5. Did the water stay in a drop or did it spread out on the slide?

15-5. It stayed in a drop.

B. Fill the jar with water. Add food coloring and stir. Then put the capillary tube halfway into the water to allow water to enter. Take the tube out of the water.

✔ 15–6. What happened to the water in the tube when the tube was removed from the jar?

15-6. The water stayed in the tube.

What you observed in Steps A and B are the results of forces called *cohesion* and *adhesion.* Cohesion was demonstrated with the water droplet and the microscope slide. The *like* molecules of the water attracted each other; the water droplet retained its shape.

ADVANCED 61

Adhesion was demonstrated with the water and the capillary tube. The *unlike* molecules of the tube and the water attracted each other; the water stayed in the tube.

15-7. Cohesion is an attraction between *like* molecules, adhesion between *unlike* molecules.

✔ 15–7. Explain the difference between cohesion and adhesion.

Figure 15–2 shows water molecules within the xylem tube.

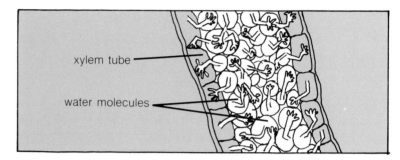

xylem tube

water molecules

Figure 15–2

15-8. The water molecules are held in the xylem tubes due to the attraction of the water molecules to each other (cohesion) and the attraction of the water and tube molecules to each other (adhesion).

★ 15–8. Describe the roles played by cohesion and adhesion in moving water through plants.

The forces of cohesion and adhesion alone do not move water in plants. But these forces do explain how the water stays in the xylem tube.

Two other factors, *root pressure* and *transpiration,* affect the movement of water in plants. Root pressure is the result of the *diffusion* of water from the soil into plant roots. A magnified cross-section of a root is shown in Figure 15–3.

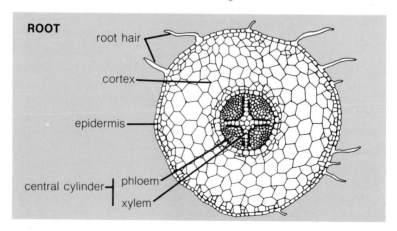

ROOT

root hair

cortex

epidermis

central cylinder — phloem

xylem

Figure 15–3

62 ADVANCED

15-9. Because there is a lower concentration of water molecules in the root hairs than there is in the surrounding soil.

✔ 15-9. A plant takes in minerals from the soil through root hairs. Then water diffuses into the root hairs. Why?

If you can't answer Question 15-9 do *Resource Unit 12.* Don't go any further until you understand diffusion.

Once water molecules are in the root hairs, they diffuse into the xylem. The continual movement of water into the root xylem creates root pressure.

A ROOT-PRESSURE DEMONSTRATION

1 Start with a healthy plant.

2 Cut off the stem above the soil. Fasten a glass tube over the cut stem.

3 Later, water rises in the glass tube.

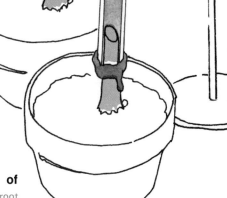

tube

water

stem

Figure 15–4

★ **15–10. Look at Figure 15–4. What causes the rise of water in the glass tube?** 15-10. The diffusion of water into the root hairs and up through the stem i.e., root pressure.

Root pressure "pushes" water up into the plant. At the same time, a process called *transpiration* creates a "pull" on the water already in the xylem. During transpiration water diffuses to and evaporates through leaf openings called *stomata* [STOW-mata]. (A single leaf opening is called a *stoma.*) Then more water can diffuse up through the xylem to replace the evaporated water.

Different plants transpire at different rates. A full-grown apple tree loses about 15 litres (16 quarts) of water every hour. A corn plant loses about 200 litres (212 quarts) of water in one growing season.

Some students may want to set up their own root-pressure demonstration.

Figure 15–5 summarizes how water moves through plants by cohesion, adhesion, root pressure, and transpiration.

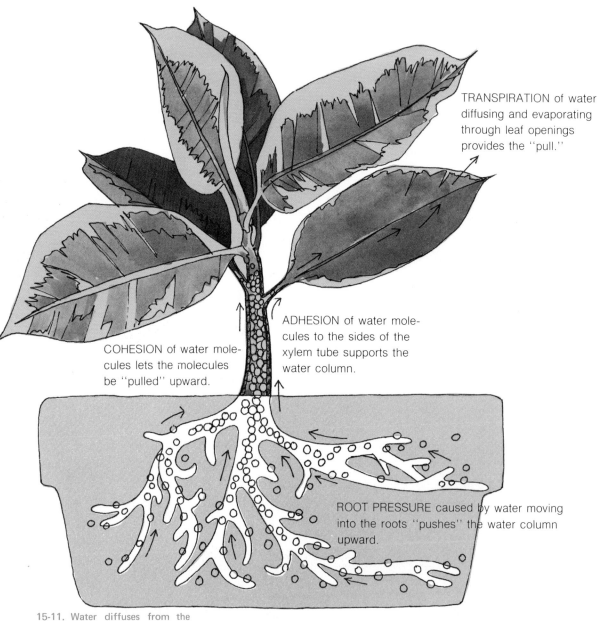

TRANSPIRATION of water diffusing and evaporating through leaf openings provides the "pull."

ADHESION of water molecules to the sides of the xylem tube supports the water column.

COHESION of water molecules lets the molecules be "pulled" upward.

ROOT PRESSURE caused by water moving into the roots "pushes" the water column upward.

Figure 15–5

15-11. Water diffuses from the soil into the root hairs and from the root hairs up into the xylem tubes (root pressure). The water is "held" in the xylem tubes by means of cohesion and adhesion. The water transpires through the leaves which results in a lower concentration of water molecules in the leaves than in the stems.

★ **15-11. Look at Figure 15–5. Describe how plants move water from roots to leaves.**

64 ADVANCED

This creates a "pull" upward on the water in the xylem.

excursion

Potpourri

Activity **18** Page 68

Certain symptoms indicate when a plant is rootbound. In this activity you'll learn to identify these symptoms. You'll also learn how to repot, clean, and humidify house plants.

Activity **16** Planning

For Activity 19 you'll make one or more plant cuttings. It will take time for the cuttings to root. So if you plan to do Activity 19, do it first.

More on Propagation

Activity **19** Page 73

There are many methods for propagating house plants. You might like to try one, two, or all three methods presented in this activity.

Make Your Own Potting Soil

Activity **17** Page 66

Do you know what the ingredients are for a general purpose potting soil? You'll find out in this activity when you make your own potting soil.

Plant Blunders

Activity **20** Page 76

This activity is a review of how *not* to take care of house plants. You'll get a chance to identify poor treatments and to prescribe the correct treatments.

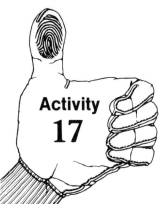

Make Your Own Potting Soil

Activity 17

A good potting soil must meet the four requirements shown in Figure 17–1. Having a good soil is critical to the health of house plants.

MATERIALS PER STUDENT UNIT
garden soil (loam), 1 litre
organic matter (peat moss or leaf mold), 1 litre
drainage materials (sand or perlite), 1 litre
fertilizer (5-10-5 or 12-6-6), 7-8 ml
superphosphate (20%), 5 ml
ground limeston, 10 ml
plastic bucket or bag
mixing stick or spoon
measuring container, 1 litre
measuring spoon, 5-ml

See Advance Preparation, page TM 9, for hints about measuring and storing the potting soil.

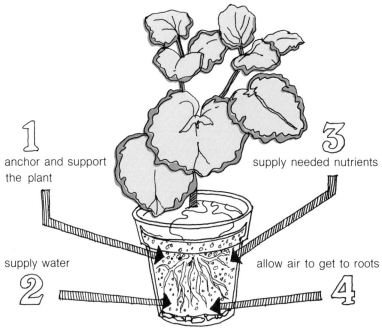

1 anchor and support the plant

3 supply needed nutrients

2 supply water

4 allow air to get to roots

Figure 17–1

In this activity you'll make potting soil. These are the materials you'll need:

    garden soil (loam), 1 litre
    organic matter (peat moss or leaf mold), 1 litre
    drainage materials (coarse builder's sand or perlite), 1 litre
    superphosphate (20%), 5 ml
    fertilizer (5-10-5 or 12-6-6), 7–8 ml
    ground limestone, 10 ml
    plastic bucket
    mixing stick or spoon
    measuring container, 1-litre
    measuring spoon, 5-ml

FIRST: MIX TOGETHER

1 litre organic matter

1 litre garden soil

1 litre drainage materials

makes about 3 litres potting soil

SECOND: ADD

5 ml superphosphate + 7–8 ml fertilizer + 10 ml ground limestone

MIX EVERYTHING WELL

If all the potting soil ingredients came from a gardening store, your soil is already sterile. If not, you'll have to heat the soil to kill pests, fungi, and weed seeds. Put the soil in a heat-resistant covered container. Preheat an oven to 82°C (180°F). Then place the container in the oven for 30 minutes. When the soil cools, it will be ready to use.

Indoor plants might grow in regular outdoor-type soil. But they'll do better in specially mixed potting soil.

✔ 17–1. The organic matter used in potting soil is soft and spongy. What will this do for the soil? (Hint: Look at Figure 17–1 again.)

17-1. It will help store water.

As organic matter decays, it supplies the plant with nutrients. But organic matter makes the soil acidic. Ground limestone reduces the amount of acid.

✔ 17–2. Why is drainage material added to the potting soil?

17-2. To allow air to get to the roots.

17-3. Because there is fertilizer in the soil mixture.

✔ 17–3. Plants potted in a good soil mixture won't need fertilizing for three to six months. Why not?

★ 17–4. What are the ingredients of a good potting soil? What is the function of each ingredient?

17-4. *Garden soil* (loam) — provides nutrients, anchors and supports the plant. *Organic matter* — holds water, provides nutrients. *Drainage material* — helps air get to roots, helps water to drain. *Ground limestone* — reduces the amount of acid in the soil. *Superphosphate* and *fertilizer* — provide nutrients.

If you plan to do Activities 18 or 19, you'll use the soil you made here. Find a place to store the soil until you need it.

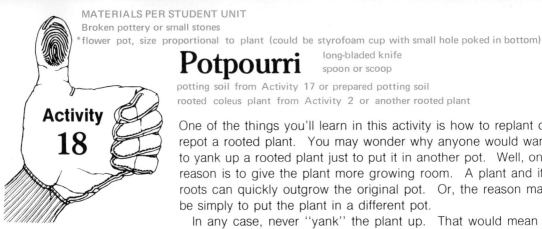

MATERIALS PER STUDENT UNIT
Broken pottery or small stones
*flower pot, size proportional to plant (could be styrofoam cup with small hole poked in bottom)
long-bladed knife
spoon or scoop
potting soil from Activity 17 or prepared potting soil
rooted coleus plant from Activity 2 or another rooted plant

Potpourri

Activity 18

One of the things you'll learn in this activity is how to replant or repot a rooted plant. You may wonder why anyone would want to yank up a rooted plant just to put it in another pot. Well, one reason is to give the plant more growing room. A plant and its roots can quickly outgrow the original pot. Or, the reason may be simply to put the plant in a different pot.

In any case, never "yank" the plant up. That would mean a quick and sure death for the plant. Study Figure 18–1. It shows four potting cautions.

POTTING CAUTIONS

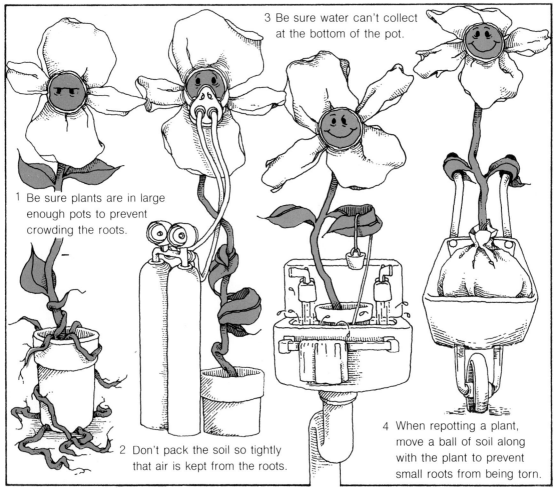

3 Be sure water can't collect at the bottom of the pot.

1 Be sure plants are in large enough pots to prevent crowding the roots.

2 Don't pack the soil so tightly that air is kept from the roots.

4 When repotting a plant, move a ball of soil along with the plant to prevent small roots from being torn.

Figure 18–1

ACTIVITY EMPHASIS: Students investigate the proper procedures for potting and repotting plants. They learn to recognize the symptoms for rootbound plants as well as how to humidify and clean plants.

*If students are allowed to keep their repotted plants, you may want them to provide their own flower pots.

68 EXCURSION

Keep the potting cautions in mind as you repot a plant. You'll need these materials:

piece of broken pottery or small stones
flower pot
potting soil from Activity 17 or prepared potting soil
rooted coleus plant from Activity 2 or another rooted plant
long-bladed knife
spoon or scoop

A. Set up the pot as shown in the drawing. Then loosen the soil around the plant by running a knife around the inside of the pot.

2 cm potting soil

broken pottery or stones

B. Look at the drawing to see how to hold the plant. Slide the plant out of the pot while supporting the root ball with a spoon. Carefully set the root ball in the new pot and add potting soil to the pot.

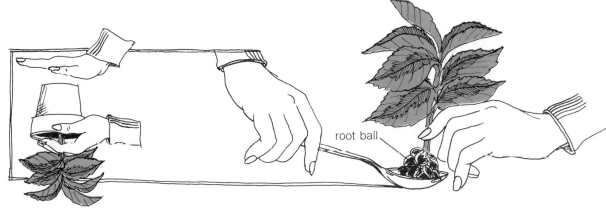

root ball

Water the soil until the water runs out the drainage hole. Keep the plant out of direct sunlight for about two weeks. Then return the plant to its normal lighting and watering.

✔ 18–1. In Step B you used the spoon to keep the old ball of soil intact. Why do you think this is important?

It is common practice to place stones or pieces of broken pottery in the bottom of a pot. This helps to keep the soil well drained.

✔ 18–2. Why should you avoid using a pot that has no opening for drainage?

★ 18–3. What are the important steps to follow when repotting a plant?

Repotting is necessary when your plant is *rootbound* or *potbound*. How do you know when a plant is rootbound? Here are some symptoms.

18-1. To keep the roots from being torn and broken.

18-2. A pot without a drainage hole will collect water. Then air can't get to the roots.

18-3. *a.* Prepare the new pot: cover the hole with drainage materials and add some potting soil.
b. Loosen the soil around the root ball of the plant. Remove the plant from the pot.
c. Supporting the root ball, place the plant in the new pot. Add soil around the sides of the ball. Water the soil until water runs out the drainage hole.

ROOTBOUND SYMPTOMS

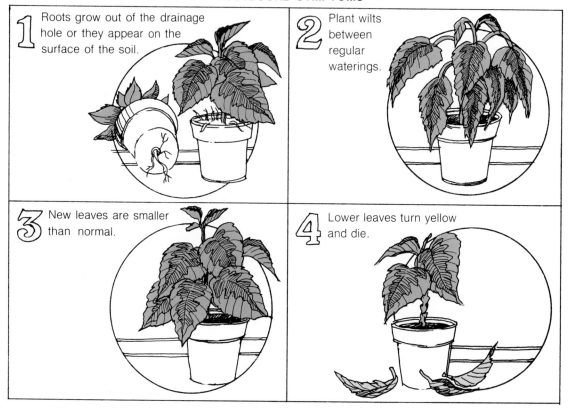

1 Roots grow out of the drainage hole or they appear on the surface of the soil.

2 Plant wilts between regular waterings.

3 New leaves are smaller than normal.

4 Lower leaves turn yellow and die.

If you still can't tell whether a plant is rootbound, you'll have to check its roots.

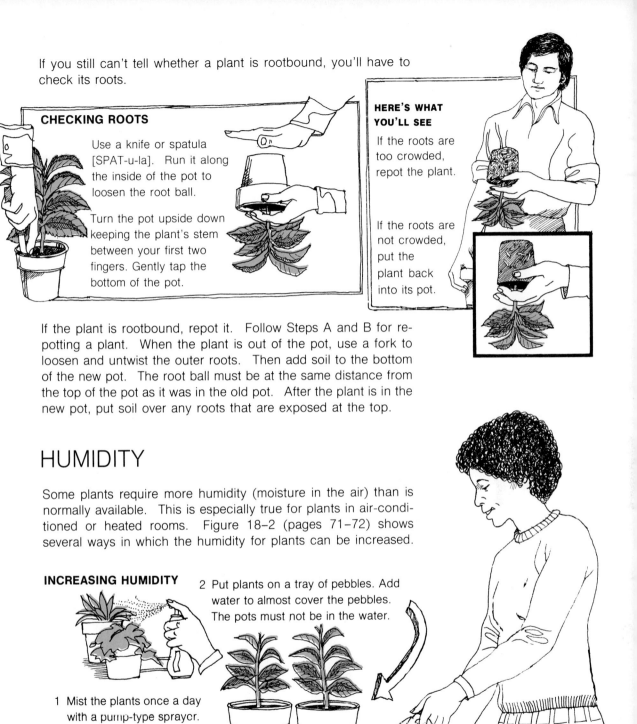

CHECKING ROOTS

Use a knife or spatula [SPAT-u-la]. Run it along the inside of the pot to loosen the root ball.

Turn the pot upside down keeping the plant's stem between your first two fingers. Gently tap the bottom of the pot.

HERE'S WHAT YOU'LL SEE

If the roots are too crowded, repot the plant.

If the roots are not crowded, put the plant back into its pot.

If the plant is rootbound, repot it. Follow Steps A and B for repotting a plant. When the plant is out of the pot, use a fork to loosen and untwist the outer roots. Then add soil to the bottom of the new pot. The root ball must be at the same distance from the top of the pot as it was in the old pot. After the plant is in the new pot, put soil over any roots that are exposed at the top.

HUMIDITY

Some plants require more humidity (moisture in the air) than is normally available. This is especially true for plants in air-conditioned or heated rooms. Figure 18–2 (pages 71–72) shows several ways in which the humidity for plants can be increased.

INCREASING HUMIDITY

2 Put plants on a tray of pebbles. Add water to almost cover the pebbles. The pots must not be in the water.

1 Mist the plants once a day with a pump-type sprayer.

Figure 18–2

3 Put a number of plants close together.

Figure 18–2

4 Put the plants in the kitchen or bathroom near the sink.

★ **18–4. Look at Figure 18–2. How does the procedure in Drawing 2 increase the humidity?**

18-4. The water in the tray evaporates, increasing the humidity in the immediate area.

CLEANING

Most plants benefit when their leaves are cleaned every two or three weeks. Several ways to clean a plant's leaves are shown in Figure 18–3.

1 Spray small plants in the sink; large plants in the shower. Use warm water. Spray both sides of leaf.

Figure 18–3

2 Dip a soft cloth in warm water and wash the leaves of the plant. Support the leaf with one hand while cleaning with the other.

3 Hold small fuzzy-leaved plants upside down and swish in warm soapy (non-detergent) water. Swish in warm water to rinse.

18-5. In clean leaves, carbon dioxide and oxygen can enter and exit easily during photosynthesis and respiration.

✔ 18–5. Why are clean leaves good for a plant?

18-6. Rubber tree plants have large leaves. Method 2 of Figure 18-3 probably will work best.

★ **18–6. How would you clean the leaves of a rubber tree plant?**

More on Propagation

In this activity you'll learn three ways to propagate (reproduce) new plants from old by taking cuttings. You may want to try one or more of these methods. For each cutting you make, you'll need the materials listed in Activity 2. If you try a vein cutting, you'll need 5 hairpins or about 20 centimeters of fine wire.

LEAF CUTTINGS

ACTIVITY EMPHASIS: Students investigate how to propagate new plants by making leaf cuttings, leaf section cuttings, and vein cuttings.

This method of propagation can be used for small indoor house plants: rex begonia, African violet, gloxinia, and peperomia.

Do Steps A and B from Activity 2. Then do the following steps, Steps C and D.

C. Remove a healthy leaf by making a diagonal cut near the bottom of the stalk.

MATERIALS PER STUDENT UNIT
Same as Activity 2 plus:
5 hair pins or 5 pieces of fine wire, 4 cm each
1 healthy plant for each type of cutting

If students plan to take their plants home, you may want them to provide their own flower pots.

D. Dip the stalk of the leaf into rooting hormone powder. Tap off the excess powder. Place the stalk into the rooting medium in the pot. Then press the medium around the stalk so that the leaf is firmly supported.

Caution: Too much rooting hormone sometimes causes rotting of herbacious plant stems.

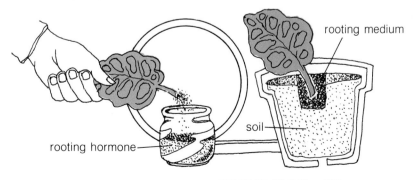

rooting medium

rooting hormone

soil

Do Step E in Activity 2, then do Step F below.

F. Put the pot in a brightly lighted place, but not in direct sunlight. Check the cutting every 2 or 3 days. When new leaves appear, the cutting has rooted. (This will be in 2 to 3 weeks.) Carefully remove the plastic.

LEAF SECTION CUTTINGS

This method of propagation can be used for a rex begonia or a wax begonia. To begin, turn to Activity 2 and do Steps A and B. In Step B, dig 3 or 4 different holes rather than 1 hole. Then do the following steps, *G* and *H*.

G. Remove a healthy leaf by making a diagonal cut near the bottom of the stalk. Cut the leaf into long sections. Make sure the base of each section has a large vein and part of the stem.

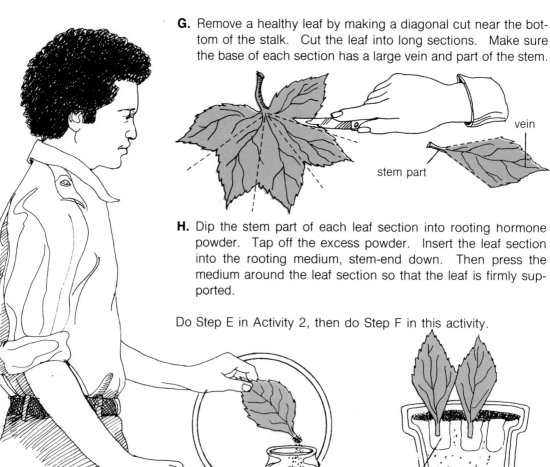

vein

stem part

H. Dip the stem part of each leaf section into rooting hormone powder. Tap off the excess powder. Insert the leaf section into the rooting medium, stem-end down. Then press the medium around the leaf section so that the leaf is firmly supported.

Do Step E in Activity 2, then do Step F in this activity.

rooting hormone

rooting medium

VEIN CUTTINGS

This method of propagation does not always work. But it is most successful with an African violet or a rex begonia. Besides the materials listed in Activity 2, you'll need the following:

  4 or 5 hairpins or about 20 cm very fine wire

First, turn to Activity 2 and do Steps A and B. In Step B dig the hole near the *side* of the pot. Then do the following steps, *I* and *J*.

I. Remove a healthy leaf by making a diagonal cut near the bottom of the stalk. Turn the leaf to the side that has clearly visible veins. Make 5 or 6 small cuts as in the drawing.

J. Place the leaf, vein-side up, in the pot. Push the leaf's stem into the rooting medium. Then use hairpins to hold down the leaf's edges.

19-1. *a.* Prepare the pot: put potting soil in the pot; dig a hole in the soil and fill it with rooting medium. Cut a leaf from the stem; dip the stalk of the leaf into rooting-hormone powder; insert the stalk in the rooting medium in the soil. Cover the pot with plastic until the cutting is rooted.

    b. Prepare the pot as in *a,* but dig 3 or 4 holes in the soil and

rooting medium

Now do Step E in Activity 2. Put the pot in a brightly lighted place, but not in direct sunlight. When small plants appear in the cuts on the veins, the cuttings have rooted. The small plants should be transplanted when they are from 5 to 8 cm tall.

★ **19-1. Describe how to propagate a plant by:**
a. leaf cuttings.
b. leaf section cuttings.
c. vein cuttings.

fill with rooting medium. Remove a leaf from the stem and cut the leaf into long sections. The base of each section must have a vein and a portion of the stem. Then proceed as in *a.*

    c. Prepare the pot as in *a,* but dig the hole near the rim of the pot. Remove a leaf from the plant. Turn the leaf vein-side up. Make small cuts across the veins. Push the leaf stalk into the rooting medium in the soil. Anchor the leaf with hair pins or fine wire. Then cover the pot with plastic until small plants are formed.

Plant Blunders

20-1. *a.* Overwatering. Use less water and/or water less often; follow watering suggestions in the *Plant Directory*. *b.* Overcrowded roots. Repot the plant in a larger pot. *c.* Roots are being ripped and broken. When repotting, keep the root ball intact.

ACTIVITY EMPHASIS: Students identify the mistakes illustrated and then describe how to correct or prevent the mistakes.

MATERIALS PER STUDENT UNIT
None.

★ 2–1. Each of the following illustrations shows a mistake. Briefly describe the mistake and tell how to correct or prevent it. If you have trouble, refer to the activity listed.

d. Too much light. Move plant to an area with less light.

e. The plant is in a drafty or cold place. Move it to a less drafty or warmer location.

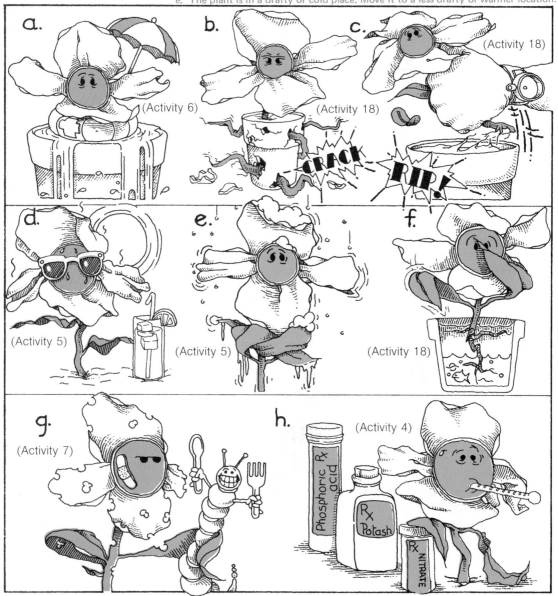

a. (Activity 6)

b. (Activity 18)

c. (Activity 18)

CRACK

RIP!

d. (Activity 5)

e. (Activity 5)

f. (Activity 18)

g. (Activity 7)

h. (Activity 4)

Phosphoric acid

Rx Potash

Rx NITRATE

f. The pot has no drainage hole. The roots can't get air. Use a pot with one or more drainage holes.

BCDEFGHIJK 07987
PRINTED IN THE UNITED STATES OF AMERICA

g. The plant is infested with pests. Isolate the plant, identify the pest, and treat accordingly.

h. Not enough fertilizer. Fertilize plant.